The Teachers & Writers Guide to Walt Whitman

The Teachers & Writers Guide

to

Walt Whitman

Edited by Ron Padgett

Teachers & Writers Collaborative
New York

The Teachers & Writers Guide to Walt Whitman

Permissions

The front cover photograph is from the collection of the National Archives, Washington, D.C. The Whitman cigar box label is from the private collection of Ron and Patricia Padgett. A different version of Allen Ginsberg's "Taking a Walk through *Leaves of Grass*" appeared as "Allen Ginsberg on Walt Whitman: Composed on the Tongue" in *Walt Whitman: The Measure of His Song*, eds. Jim Perlman, Ed Folsom, and Dan Campion (Holy Cow! Press, 1981). Revised version *(cont. p. 208)*

Teachers & Writers Collaborative
5 Union Square West
New York, NY 10003
(212) 691-6590

Library of Congress Cataloging-in-Publication Data

The Teachers & writers guide to Walt Whitman / edited by Ron Padgett.
       p.   cm.
    Includes bibliographical references.
    ISBN 0–915924–36-6 (paper)
    1. Whitman, Walt, 1819–1892—Study and teaching. 2. Whitman, Walt, 1819–1892—Criticism and interpretation. I. Padgett, Ron. II. Title: Teachers & writers guide to Walt Whitman.
PS3238.T4 1991
811'.3—dc20   91–2778
                                     CIP

Second printing

Cover design by Trevor Winkfield & Ron Padgett
Printed by Philmark Lithographics, New York, N.Y.

Table of Contents

Table of Illustrations

Acknowledgments

The editor wishes to express his thanks to the authors who wrote new material for this book: Kenneth Koch, Larry Fagin, Dale Worsley, William Bryant Logan, Anne Waldman, Mark Statman, Bill Zavatsky, Gary Lenhart, Margot Fortunato Galt, and Jack Collom; and to the people who offered advice on this project: Nancy Shapiro, Patricia Padgett, Chris Edgar, Simon Kilmurry, Trevor Winkfield, and Jessica Sager of Teachers & Writers Collaborative; Bill Berkson and John Oliver Simon, poets; Joan Wilmarth and Kim Niemela of the Walt Whitman Association; Barbara Doris Vlahides of the New York University Humanities Council; Rick Beard and Andrew Svedlow of the Museum of the City of New York; Mina R. Weiner, coordinator of the Walt Whitman Festival; Kathy Condon of South Street Seaport; Frank Murphy of Smith College; David Reynolds of City University of New York; Beth McCabe and William Wadsworth of the Academy of American Poets; Jane McDonough of the Brooklyn Historical Society; Joanne Krieg of Hofstra University; Ed Folsom of the University of Iowa; Jim Perlman of Holy Cow! Press; Galway Kinnell of New York University; the staff of the New York Public Library; Bonnie Wilson of the Minnesota Historical Society; Elsie T. Freeman, Chief of the Education Branch of the National Archives, Washington, D.C.; and the staffs of the Walt Whitman Birthplace in Huntington, Long Island, and Harleigh Cemetery in Camden, New Jersey.

•

Teachers & Writers Collaborative is very grateful for current support from the New York State Council on the Arts, National Endowment for the Arts, Aaron Diamond Foundation, American Stock Exchange, Mr. Bingham's Trust for Charity, Chemical Bank, Consolidated Edison, DeWitt Wallace-Reader's Digest Fund, Joelson Foundation, Louis Calder Foundation, Manufacturers Hanover Trust Company, Morgan Stanley Foundation, New York Rotary Foundation, New York Telephone, New York Times Company Foundation, Henry Nias Foundation, Helena Rubinstein Foundation, the Scherman Foundation, and Steele-Reese Foundation, as well as individual members of Teachers & Writers Collaborative.

Teachers & Writers is also grateful to past support from American Airlines, American Broadcasting Companies, American Can Company Foundation, AT&T Long Lines, Vincent Astor Foundation, Atari Institute for Educational Action Research, Avon Products Foundation, Bankers Trust Company, Chase Manhattan Bank, CBS, Inc., Citibank, Columbia Committee for Community Service, Equitable Life Assurance Society, Exxon Education Foundation, Field Foundation, Ford Foundation, Fund for Poetry, General Electric Foundation, Herman Goldman Foundation, Edward W. Hazen Foundation, Heckscher Foundation for Children, Hugh Hefner Foundation, International Paper Company Foundation, KIDS Fund, Kulchur Foundation, Long Island Community Trust, Mobil Foundation, Morgan Guaranty Trust Company, New York Community Trust, New York Foundation, Newsweek, Overseas Shipholding Group, J.C. Penney Company, Ellis L. Phillips Foundation, Pisces Foundation, RCA, Surdna Foundation, and Variety Club of New York.

•

Finally, because the first edition of this book is being published on the occasion of the twenty-fifth anniversary of Teachers & Writers Collaborative, we would like to salute our visionary founders and the many writers and artists who have taken part in our program.

Preface

by Ron Padgett

> *I contain multitudes.*
> —Whitman

This book grew out of conversations at Teachers & Writers Collaborative about ways to celebrate the work of Walt Whitman on the centenary of his death. We asked poets and fiction writers to tell us of interesting ways not only to read Whitman, but also to write prose and poetry inspired by his work. Much of his writing has remained remarkably fresh, and our hope is that the current volume will send readers back to it for the kind of give-and-take that Whitman himself welcomed.

His work is extraordinarily friendly and informal. Unlike his three-name contemporaries (Henry Wadsworth Longfellow, Ralph Waldo Emerson, James Whitcomb Riley, etc.), he is simply "Walt" Whitman. The distinction becomes clearer when we try to imagine a "Hank" Longfellow or a "Jim" Riley. So far as I know, Whitman was the first American poet to publish under an informal name. He may have wanted to avoid identifying with his father (Walter Whitman, Sr.) or being relegated to "junior" status. Regardless, his calling himself Walt goes hand in hand with his being "the poet of democracy," with shirt unbuttoned and sleeves rolled up, extolling the open air, comradeship, and the optimism of a young America. Whitman's poetry is indeed attractive and easy to like, but it is also subtler and more literary—without seeming to be—than people often say it is. It has depth and resonance.

Such resonance is lacking in his most anthologized poem, "O Captain! My Captain!" about which Whitman himself later said, "I'm almost sorry I ever wrote the poem." He could be windy, too. In fact, he wrote quite a lot of undistinguished fiction, newspaper articles, and poetry before he became the poet we think of as Walt Whitman. According to many of his employers, he was indolent: he liked to "loafe," to go off and walk around and sit or lie down and look at things and let them sink in slowly. For him, writing and loafing were an ideal combination. The great, continuing mystery is how he went from being a thoroughly

TRADE MARK REGISTERED

Fig. 1: Cigar box label (Whitman didn't smoke).

pedestrian writer to being a great poet. For all of us who write or teach writing, it is an example that gives us hope.

What's the best edition of Whitman? The reader looking for the one perfect edition will find a bewildering, marvelous variety to choose from. There isn't even a single *Leaves of Grass*. Over a period of around forty years, Whitman rewrote, cut, and expanded it; the first edition (1855) contained 12 poems, the last (1892) 383. Although his revisions over the years tended to dull the freshness and energy of the first edition, he did add some great new poems. Various editors, having a number of Whitmans to choose from, have produced different editions of his work (see the Whitman Resources section for annotations on some of those currently available). Whitman afficionados bypass the dilemma simply by getting all the editions they can. However, anyone looking for one all-purpose, inexpensive edition would do well to choose *The Portable Walt Whitman*, edited by Mark Van Doren, which includes a major portion of *Leaves of Grass* (including the text of the original edition), a healthy chunk of Whitman's prose (the complete *Specimen Days*, for example), an introduction, chronology, and bibliography. The *Portable* was lab-tested at Teachers & Writers: it *almost* fits into a blue jeans hip pocket.

Not surprisingly, the contributors to the present volume have based their essays on different editions. For the sake of the reader's convenience, I have tried to make their references correlate to the *Portable*, but in some cases it wasn't possible. For instance, Allen Ginsberg's piece was structured on his taking a verbal walk through an out-of-print Modern Library edition of *Leaves of Grass*. When I asked him why he used that edition, he said, "It's just the one I've had all these years." I go back to yet another Modern Library *Leaves*—even knowing that it's not a very good text—because it's the Whitman I happened to buy when I was sixteen. Reading Whitman tends to be a personal experience.

Different writers also have different ideas about how to teach Whitman. The general idea of this volume is not to have the teacher try to turn his or her students (or self) into miniature Walt Whitmans, but rather to give them ways to get close enough to his work so that some of its energy can transfer to them, an energy capable of propelling them toward a stronger sense of themselves, toward what Muriel Rukeyser called "basic rhythms":

Out of [Whitman's] own body, and its relation to itself and the sea, he drew his basic rhythms. They are not the rhythms, as has been asserted, of work and love-making; but rather of the relation of our breathing to our heartbeat, and these measured against an ideal of water at the shore, not beginning nor ending, but endlessly drawing in, making forever its forms of massing and falling among the breakers, seething in the white recessions of its surf, never finishing, always making a meeting-place. ("Whitman and the Problem of Good" in *The Life of Poetry* [New York: Current Books, Inc., A. A. Wyn Publisher, 1949])

Few of us have grown up that close to an ocean; we have the plains, the mountains, the woods, the town, or the city in our blood, hence the "basic rhythms" among us show great range. The contributors to the current volume demonstrate such range.

Allen Ginsberg's essay—an edited transcript of a spontaneous talk—is a broad, personal overview of Whitman as a man, poet, and visionary of democracy. Kenneth Koch takes apart the first five lines of "Song of Myself" and puts them back together. Jim Berger offers ways to teach poetry writing based on Whitman's long line. In the next five essays, poets describe how they have used particular poems to inspire student writing: Kenneth Koch ("Song of Myself"), Larry Fagin ("I Hear America Singing"), Dale Worsley ("A Child Went Forth"), William Bryant Logan ("The Sleepers"), and Anne Waldman (also "The Sleepers"). Mark Statman's "Poet of the Crowd" talks about some of the particular effects of reading Whitman. William Bryant Logan's "Whitman's Own Way: The Poet as Role Model" is particularly heartening for teachers of adolescents. Bill Zavatsky discusses teaching Whitman in high school, but manages to pull in a lot of other ideas and information. My note on Whitman as a teacher is followed by three articles on education by Whitman himself. Allen Ginsberg then remembers the high school teacher who helped imprint Whitman "on [his] head." Langston Hughes's essay manages to give us the essence of Whitman in just a few pages. The emphasis shifts to Whitman as prose writer and as informal historian in Gary Lenhart's essay. Margot Fortunato Galt combines the study of history and the writing of poetry in her piece. Jack Collom's essay discusses a Whitman poem in the context of ecology, confirming once again the variousness of Whitman's work. Throughout these essays are many examples of poems by students from kindergarten through college. Fol lowing Collom's piece is a little grab bag of teaching ideas I assembled. Dave Morice's Whitman cartoon rounds out the main body of this book in a work that manages to be both serious and funny at the same time. The Whitman Resources section describes some of the good materials currently available for Whitman studies: books, magazines, graphic materials, audiotapes, and videotapes, as well as places to visit.

There are, of course, other ways of learning about Whitman. For example, Galway Kinnell feels that the best way to learn about Whitman's style is simply to memorize long passages, in order to see the poems from the inside, to understand the poet's decisions better.

Finally, although some of the essays in this book provide exercises and suggestions for English, creative writing, history, social studies, journalism, and ecology classrooms, there is no reason the reader cannot assume that the world is a classroom, and that teacher and student sometimes are aspects of the same person. The aim of the present volume is not to be comprehensive, but to give readers a fresh look at Whitman by pointing them in directions we have found to be inspiring, interesting, and useful. This book is an invitation for you to take your own walk alongside this marvelous poet.

Taking a Walk through *Leaves of Grass*

by Allen Ginsberg

There was a man, Walt Whitman, who lived in the nineteenth century, in America, who began to define his own person, who began to tell his own secrets, who outlined his own body, and made an outline of his own mind, so other people could see it. He was sort of the prophet of American democracy in the sense that he got to be known as the "good gray poet" when he got to be an old, old man because he was so honest and so truthful and at the same time so enormous-voiced and bombastic. As he said: "I sound my barbaric yawp over the roofs of the world," writing in New York City probably then, thinking of the skyline and roofs of Manhattan as it might have been in 1853 or so. He began announcing himself, and announcing person, with a big capital *P*, Person, self, or one's own nature, one's own original nature, what you really think when you're alone in bed, after everybody's gone home from the party or when you're looking in the mirror, shaving, or when you're not shaving and you're looking in the mirror, looking at your long, white, aged beard, or if you're sitting on the toilet, or thinking to yourself, "What happened to life? What happened to Mommy?" or if you're just walking down the street, looking at people full of longing.

So he wrote a book called *Leaves of Grass.*** And, in the final version of that book, the very first inscription was:

One's-self I sing, a simple separate person,
Yet utter the word Democratic, the word En-Masse.
Of physiology from top to toe I sing,
Not physiognomy alone nor brain alone is worthy for the Muse, I say
    the Form complete is worthier far,
The Female equally with the Male I sing.
Of Life immense in passion, pulse, and power,

---

* The text referred to here is from *Leaves of Grass and Selected Prose* (New York: Modern Library, Random House, Inc., 1950) edited by John Kouwenhoven. Page numbers from this edition appear in parentheses after most citations.

1

Cheerful, for freest action form'd under the laws divine,
The modern man I sing. (p. 3)

Well, that's kind of interesting. He starts with the female equally with the male, so he begins in the middle of the nineteenth century by talking about "women's lib": "The Female equally with the Male I sing." But he also says he's going to talk about the body, about physiology from top to toe, he's going to sing about the toes and the hair: modern man. This is on the very first page.

Then, further on, he has a little note, "To Foreign Lands":

I heard that you ask'd for something to prove this puzzle the New World,
And to define America, her athletic Democracy,
Therefore I send you my poems that you behold in them what you wanted. (p. 5)

An "athletic Democracy," what does he mean by that? He means people who are able to get up off their ass and get out and look up at the blue sky in the middle of the night and realize how big the universe is and how little, tiny America is, or how vast our souls are, and how small this state is, or the Capitol building, magnificent and glorious as it is, how it's rendered the size of an ant's forefoot by the immensity of a cloud above it. And so, the soul that sees the cloud above the Capitol or the universe above the cloud is the giant athletic soul, you could almost say. It's democracy, though, that is the key, which for him means, in the long run, the love of comrades, that men will love men, women will love women, men will love women, women will love men, that there will be a spontaneous tenderness between them as the basis of the democracy.

So he goes on, "To the States," announcing:

To the States or any one of them, or any city of the States, *Resist much, obey little*
Once unquestioning obedience, once fully enslaved,
Once fully enslaved, no nation, state, city of this earth, ever afterward resumes its liberty. (p. 9)

That's a warning to America, much needed later on, as when Eisenhower, the president a hundred years later, warned: Watch out for the military-industrial complex which demands unques-

2

tioning obedience and slavery to military aggression. Fear, nuclear apocalypse, unquestioning obedience like "Don't ask, maybe they know better than you do." So this is a warning from Whitman about the difficulties of democracy. Then he, like a bodhisattva, that is to say, someone who has taken a vow to enlighten all beings in all the directions of space and in all the three times—past, present, and future—has a little poem or song to his fellow poets that would be born after him, who, like myself, will sit in a recording studio reading his words aloud to be heard by ears through some kind of movie/television/theater:

Poets to come! orators, singers, musicians to come!
Not today is to justify me and answer what I am for,
But you, a new brood, native, athletic, continental, greater than
     before known,
Arouse! for you must justify me.

I myself but write one or two indicative words for the future,
I but advance a moment only to wheel and hurry back in the dark-
     ness.

I am a man who, sauntering along without fully stopping, turns a
     casual look upon you and then averts his face,
Leaving it to you to prove and define it,
Expecting the main things from you. (p. 12)

Ah, there's some suggestion here that Whitman wants somebody to pick him up in the street and make love to him. But he wants to give that glance so that you know he's open, but what kind of love does he want?

He wants a democratic love, and he wants an athletic love, he wants a love from men too, and he also wants a love in the imagination. He wants an expansiveness, he wants communication, he wants some kind of vow that everybody will cherish each other sacramentally. So he's going to make the first breakthrough—that's what he's saying. So he's got another little poem following that, "To You":

Stranger, if you passing meet me and desire to speak to me, why
     should you not speak to me?
And why should I not speak to you? (p. 12)

Well, I don't know why not, except everybody's too scared to

3

speak to strangers in the street, they might get hit for being thought a fairy or a nut talking in the subway or babbling to himself in the street. But Whitman was willing to talk to anybody, he said. Of course, he was living in a time when there was less fear.

His major work is known as "Song of Myself." "Song of Myself" is a long thing, about thirty-two pages of not such big type; he wrote a lot. And this was a major statement, this was his declaration of his own nature. Now, what is a declaration of nature for a guy? In the nineteenth century, everybody was writing in closed verse forms. Some poets went to Germany for their education, like Longfellow, they went to Heidelberg University, and they studied esoteric sociology and epistemology and linguistics and ancient Greek and they thought back on the United States romantically and wrote long poems about Hiawatha and the Indian maidens under the full moon near the Canadian lakes. Whitman actually just stayed in America and slugged it out with the beer carts along the Bowery and wandered up and down and sat afternoons in Pfaff's. Pfaff's was a bar he used to go to, a Bohemian hangout, a downstairs beer hall, sort of like a German *bierstuben.* Bohemian friends used to meet there, probably like a gay gang, plus a newspaper gang, plus a theatrical gang, and the opera singers, and some of the dancers, a Broadway crowd sort of, but further down Broadway, near Bleecker. And that was his hangout.

He was very naïve at first. A young guy, he started out writing bad poetry, temperance novels, and newspaper articles, and editing the *Brooklyn Daily Eagle.* Then something happened to him in his thirties, about thirty-four—well, you know, crucifixion time—maybe he realized he was going to die someday or that America was weird, or that he was weird, or maybe some kind of breakthrough of personal affection, maybe some kind of gay lib thing. Anyway, he discovered that his own mind and his own enthusiasm, his own expansiveness is the thing, that his mind was so expansive that it was completely penetrant; because of its curiosity and inquisitiveness it penetrated every crevice and nook, every tree, bowl, every vagina, every anus, every mouth, every flower stamen, every horse's ear, every behind and cloud that he met. He wandered, he thought a lot, he wandered in his mind, and he wasn't ashamed of what he thought.

Whitman was probably the first writer in America who was not ashamed of the fact that his thoughts were as big as the universe, or that they were equal to the universe, or that they fitted the universe. He wasn't ashamed of his mind or his body. So he wrote "Song of Myself," and it began tipping off where he was coming from and where he was going, saying that you, too, needn't be ashamed of your thoughts:

I celebrate myself and sing myself,
And what I assume you shall assume,
For every atom belonging to me as good belongs to you.

I loafe and invite my soul,
I lean and loafe at my ease observing a spear of summer grass.

My tongue, every atom of my blood, form'd from this soil, this air,
Born here of parents born here from parents the same, and their
     parents the same,
I, now thirty-seven years old in perfect health begin,
Hoping to cease not till death.

Creeds and schools in abeyance,
Retiring back a while sufficed what they are, but never forgotten,
I harbor for good or bad, I permit to speak at every hazard,
Nature without check with original energy. (pp. 23–24)

Wow, what a thing to do!
    In Part 2 of "Song of Myself"—going on with his original mind that he's presenting—he looks out at the drawing rooms of Brooklyn and lower Manhattan and the rich and sophisticated culture of his day, and he sees that it's pretty shallow:

Houses and rooms are full of perfumes, the shelves are crowded with
     perfumes,
I breathe the fragrance myself and know it and like it,
The distillation would intoxicate me also, but I shall not let it.

The atmosphere is not a perfume, it has no taste of the distillation, it
     is odorless,
It is for my mouth forever, I am in love with it,
I will go to the bank by the wood and become undisguised and naked,
I am mad for it to be in contact with me.

The smoke of my own breath,
Echoes, ripples, buzz'd whispers, love-root, silk-thread, crotch and
    vine,
My respiration and inspiration, the beating of my heart, the passing
    of blood and air through my lungs,
The sniff of green leaves and dry leaves, and of the shore and dark-
    color'd sea-rocks, and of hay in the barn,
The sound of the belch'd words of my voice loos'd to the eddies of the
    wind,
A few light kisses, a few embraces, a reaching around of arms,
The play of sun and shade on the trees as the supple boughs wag,
The delight alone or in the rush of the streets, or along the fields and
    hill-sides,
The feeling of health, the full-noon trill, the song of me rising from
    bed and meeting the sun.

Have you reckon'd a thousand acres much? have you reckon'd the
    earth much?
Have you practis'd so long to learn to read?
Have you felt so proud to get at the meaning of poems?

Stop this day and night with me and you shall possess the origin of
    all poems.
You shall possess the good of the earth and sun, (there are millions
    of suns left,)
You shall no longer take things at second or third hand, nor look
    through the eyes of the dead, nor feed on the spectres in books,
You shall not look through my eyes either, nor take things from me,
You shall listen on all sides and filter them from your self. (pp. 24–
    25)

What he's done here is he has completely possessed his own body,
he's gone over and realized he's breathing, that his heart is
beating, that he has roots that go from his crotch to his brain, he
begins to sniff around him, and to extend his thought around him
to the sea, to the woods, to the cities, recognizes his emotions,
going all the way out to the millions of suns, then realizes that
most of the time we take things second- and third-hand. Who
actually looks out of their own eyes and sees the revolutions in
the trees in the fall or the bursting forth of tiny revolutions with
each grass blade? Well, Whitman looked that way and recommended that everybody else look at the actual world around
them rather than the abstract world they read about in the
newspapers or saw as a pseudo-image/event, screened dots on

television: "You shall listen on all sides and filter them from your self."

So, what is he going to do now? What is he going to say next about where we all come from, where we are going?

I have heard what the talkers were talking, the talk of the beginning
  and the end,
But I do not talk of the beginning or the end.

There was never any more inception than there is now,
Nor any more youth or age than there is now,
And will never be any more perfection than there is now,
Not any more of heaven or hell than there is now. (p. 25)

That's a great statement, very similar to what some of the Eastern, Oriental meditators, transcendentalists, or grounded Buddhists might say. Their notion is that everything is here already, wasn't born a billion years ago and slowly developed, and isn't going to be dead a billion years from now and slowly undevelop, it's just here, like a flower in the air. There's never going to be any more hell than there is right now and never going to be any more understanding of heaven than there is right now in our own minds, with our own perception. So that means you can't postpone your acceptation and realization, you can't scream at your own eyes now, you've got to look out through your own eyes, as Whitman said, hear with your own ears, smell with your own nose, touch with your own touch, fingers, taste with your own tongue, and be satisfied.

I see, dance, love, sing;
As the hugging and loving bed-fellow sleeps at my side through the
  night, and withdraws at the peep of the day with stealthy tread,
Leaving me baskets cover'd with white towels swelling the house
  with their plenty,
Shall I postpone my acceptation and realization and scream at my
  eyes,
That they turn from gazing after and down the road,
And forthwith cipher and show to me a cent,
Exactly the value of one and exactly the value of two, and which is
  ahead? (p. 26)

He's not interested in that kind of invidious comparison and competition. In the midst of "Song of Myself" he does come to a statement about the very nature of the human mind, his mind as he observed it in himself and when the mind is most open, most expanded, most realized, what relation is there between human beings and between man and nature. There are some little epiphanous moments showing, for one thing, his meditative view; for example, in the fourth part of "Song of Myself" from "Trippers and askers surround me" down to "I witness and wait." Now that's a real classical viewpoint—the last person to announce that was John Keats, who said he had a little idea about what made Shakespeare great: "negative capability." Which is to say, the possibility of seeing contending parties, seeing the Communists and Capitalists scream at each other, or the Muslims and Christians, or the Jews and the Arabs, or the self and the not-self, or your mommy and daddy, or yourself and your wife. You can see them all screaming at each other, and you can see it as a kind of comedic drama that you don't get tangled and lost in, you don't enter into the fantasy of being right and being one side or the other so completely that you go out and chop somebody's head off. Instead you just sort of watch yourself, you watch them, in and out of the game at the same time, watching and wondering at it. That is to say, the ability to have contrary ideas in your head at the same time without freaking out, without "an irritable reaching after fact" or conclusions. Because maybe you don't know the answer, maybe there is not even a question, though there may be perturbation and conflict. You are simultaneously in and out of the game, watching and wondering at it, which is the best we can do actually. The best thing we can do is wonder at everything, it's so amazing. So, then what happens? If you take that attitude and open yourself up and allow yourself to admit everything, to hear everything, not to exclude, just be like the moon in the old Japanese haiku: "The autumn moon/shines kindly/on the flower-thief," or like Whitman's sun which shines on the prostitute in his poem "To a Common Prostitute"—"Not till the sun excludes you do I exclude you." His mind is there, he's aware of her, she's aware of him and they're both internally scratching their heads. So there is an epiphany out of this, or a rise, or a kind of exquisite awareness that intensifies. Part 5 of "Song of Myself":

I believe in you my soul, the other I am must not abase itself to you,
And you must not be abased to the other.

Loafe with me on the grass, loose the stop from your throat,
Not words, not music or rhyme I want, not custom or lecture, not
    even the best,
Only the lull I like, the hum of your valved voice.

I mind how once we lay such a transparent summer morning,
How you settled your head athwart my hips and gently turn'd over
    upon me,
And parted the shirt from my bosom-bone, and plunged your tongue
    to my bare-stript heart,
And reach'd till you felt my beard, and reach'd till you held my feet.

Swiftly arose and spread around me the peace and knowledge that
    pass all argument of the earth,
And I know that the hand of God is the promise of my own,
And I know that the spirit of God is the brother of my own,
And that all the men ever born are also my brothers, and the women
    my sisters and lovers,
And that a kelson of the creation is love.
And limitless are leaves stiff or drooping in the fields,
And brown ants in the little wells beneath them,
And mossy scabs of the worn fence, heap'd stones, elder, mullein,
    and poke-weed. (p. 27)

Just out of that one experience of a touch with another person, of complete acceptance, his awareness spread throughout the space around him and he realized that that friendly touch, that friendly awareness was what bound the entire universe together and held everything suspended in gravity.

    Given this, where could he go from here? Well, the answer was a long survey of America, which he did in "Song of Myself," in which he extended his own awareness to encompass the entire basic spiritual awareness of America, trying to make an ideal America that would be an America of comradely awareness, acknowledgment of tenderness, acknowledgment of gentleness, acknowledgment of comradeship, acknowledgment of what he called adhesiveness. Because what he said was that if this country did not have some glue to keep people together, to bind them together—adhesiveness, some emotional bond—there was no possibility of democracy's working, and we'd just be a lot of separate people fighting for an advantage: military advantage, commercial advantage, iron advantage, coal advantage, silver advantage, gold advantage, even hunting up some kind of monopoly on molybdenum. On the other hand, there was the possibility of a total democracy of feeling, as in Part 11 of "Song of Myself":

Twenty-eight young men bathe by the shore,
Twenty-eight young men and all so friendly;
Twenty-eight years of womanly life and all so lonesome.

She owns the fine house by the rise of the bank,
She hides handsome and richly drest aft the blinds of the window.

Which of the young men does she like the best?
Ah the homeliest of them is beautiful to her.

Where are you off to, lady? for I see you,
You splash in the water there, yet stay stock still in your room.

Dancing and laughing along the beach came the twenty-ninth
     bather,
The rest did not see her, but she saw them and loved them.

The beards of the young men glisten'd with wet, it ran from their
     long hair,
Like streams pass'd all over their bodies.

An unseen hand also pass'd over their bodies,
It descended tremblingly from their temples and ribs.

The young men float on their backs, their white bellies bulge to the
     sun, they do not ask who seizes fast to them,
They do not know who puffs and declines with pendant and bending
     arch,
They do not think whom they souse with spray. (pp. 31–32)

Erotic tenderness is of course implicit in this longing for closeness. He pointed to that longing as basic to our bodies, basic to our minds, basic to our community, basic to our sociability, basic to our society, therefore basic to our politics. If that compassion, erotic longing, tenderness, and gentleness were squelched, repressed, pushed back, denied, insulted, mocked, seen cynically, then the entire operation of democracy would be squelched, debased, mocked, or seen cynically, made into a paranoid, mechano-megalopolis congregation of freaks afraid of each other. That process may have been the very nature of industrial civilization; the roboting of work and the homogenization of talk and thought and imagery, cause people to speak not for themselves but talk falsely, unlike Whitman, as if they represented anything but themselves. Human society has become kind of messed up; so, in Part 32 of "Song of Myself," he says:

I think I could turn and live with animals, they are so placid and
    self-contain'd,
I stand and look at them long and long.

They do not sweat and whine about their condition,
They do not lie awake in the dark and weep for their sins,
They do not make me sick discussing their duty to God,
Not one is dissatisfied, not one is demented with the mania of
    owning things,
Not one kneels to another, nor to his kind that lived thousands of
    years ago.
Not one is respectable or unhappy over the whole earth. (p. 50)

Not one animal is respectable, in all of creation. All these human beings want to be respectable, but he is pointing out that not one elephant in Africa would ever dream of considering itself respectable. So animals "show their relations to me and I accept them, they bring me tokens of myself, they evince them plainly in their possession" (p. 50).

Then, what does he do in the city? He's lonesome, so there's a little one-line description of himself in the city, "Looking in at the shop-windows on Broadway the whole forenoon, flattening the flesh of my nose on the thick plate-glass" (p. 52). But then, he can also mentally leave: "I go hunting polar-furs and the seal, leaping chasms with a pike-pointed staff, clinging to topples of brittle and blue" (p. 54). He empathizes with everybody: "I am an old artillerist, I tell of my fort's bombardment, I am there again" (p. 56). And in Part 34: "Now I will tell what I knew in Texas in my early youth" (p. 56), and then he goes on with a long anecdote. Or, in Part 35: "Would you hear of an old-time sea-fight?" (p. 58), and he goes on to telling about old-time sea-fights, and "Toward twelve there in the beams of the moon they surrender to us" (p. 59)—the moony imagination. Maybe he's a sea-fighter, or he's an Arctic explorer, or maybe he's a jerk. Part 37:

You laggards there on guard! Look to your arms!
In at the conquer'd doors they crowd! I am possess'd!
Embody all presences outlaw'd or suffering,
See myself in prison shaped like another man,
And feel the dull unintermitted pain.

For me the keepers of convicts shoulder their carbines and keep
    watch,
It is I let out in the morning and barr'd at night.

Not a mutineer walks handcuff'd to jail but I am handcuff'd to him
    and walk by his side,
(I am the less jolly one there, and more the silent one with sweat on
    my twitching lips.) (pp. 59–60)

He wasn't afraid of that—as he says: "Askers embody themselves in me and I am embodied in them, I project my hat, sit
shame-faced, and beg" (p. 59). That's like Bob Dylan in his film
Renaldo and Clara, walking down the street and all of a sudden
the camera catches him and stares him in the eye and he stares
the camera in the eye and all of a sudden he shivers and holds out
his right hand, "Some change? Spare change of love? Spare
change?" And so you have,

Enough! enough! enough!
Somehow I've been stunn'd. Stand back!
Give me a little time beyond my cuff'd head, slumbers, dreams
    gaping,
I discover myself on the verge of a usual mistake.

That I could forget the mockers and insults!
That I could forget the trickling tears and the blows of the bludgeons
    and hammers!
That I could look with a separate look on my own crucifixion and
    bloody crowning. (p. 60)

Ah, so he has suffered a bit here, he does empathize with all the
beggars, the monstrous convicts with sweat twitching on their
lips, but his point here is that everybody so suffers, everybody is
everybody else, in the sense of having experienced in imagination or in real life all of the non-respectable emotions of the
elephants and the ants. So he says, in part 44:

It is time to explain myself—let us stand up.

What is known I strip away,
I launch all men and women forward with me into the Unknown.

The clock indicates the moment—but what does eternity indicate?

We have thus far exhausted trillions of winters and summers,
There are trillions ahead, and trillions ahead of them.

Births have brought us richness and variety,
And other births will bring us richness and variety. (p. 67)

and

I am an acme of things accomplish'd, and I an encloser of things to
    be.

My feet strike the apex of the apices of the stairs,
On every step bunches of ages, and larger bunches between the
    steps,
All below duly travel'd, and still I mount and mount.

Rise after rise bow the phantoms behind me,
Afar down I see the huge first Nothing, I knew I was even there,
I waited unseen and always, and slept through the lethargic mist,
And took my time and took no hurt from the fetid carbon.
Long I was hugg'd close—long and long.

Immense have been the preparations for me,
Faithful and friendly the arms that have help'd me.

Cycles ferried my cradle, rowing and rowing like cheerful boatmen,
For room to me stars kept aside in their own rings,
They sent influences to look after what was to hold me.

Before I was born out of my mother generations guided me,
My embryo has never been torpid, nothing could overlay it.

For it the nebula cohered to an orb,
The long slow strata piled to rest it on,
Vast vegetables gave it sustenance,
Monstrous sauroids transported it in their mouths and deposited it
    with care.

13

All forces have been steadily employ'd to complete and delight me,
Now on this spot I stand with my robust soul. (pp. 67–68)

So that's great, he's here, he recognizes he's here:

My rendezvous is appointed, it is certain,
The Lord will be there and wait till I come on perfect terms,
The great Camerado, the lover true for whom I pine will be there.
   (p. 69)

So he says:

I have no chair, no church, no philosophy,
I lead no man to a dinner-table, library, exchange,
But each man and each woman of you I lead upon a knoll,
My left hand hooking you round the waist,
My right hand pointing to landscapes of continents and the public
   road.
Not I, not any one else can travel that road for you,
You must travel it for yourself.

It is not far, it is within reach,
Perhaps you have been on it since you were born and did not know,
Perhaps it is everywhere on water and on land.

Shoulder your duds, dear son, and I will mine, and let us hasten
   forth,
Wonderful cities and free nations we shall fetch as we go.

If you tire, give me both burdens, and rest the chuff of your hand on
   my hip,
And in due time you shall repay the same service to me,
For after we start we never lie by again. (pp. 69–70)

On the road, Walt Whitman prophesying what would happen to
America 100 years later.
   At the end of the poem he comes to his conclusions. He wants
to tell finally what he can get out of it all, as in Part 50 from
"There is that in me" to "It is not chaos or death—it is form,
union, plan—it is eternal life—it is Happiness" (p. 74) and in
Part 51:

The past and present wilt—I have fill'd them, emptied them,
And proceed to fill my next fold of the future.

Listener up there! What have you to confide to me?
Look in my face while I snuff the sidle of evening,
(Talk honestly, no one else hears you, and I stay only a moment
   longer.)

Do I contradict myself?
Very well then I contradict myself,
(I am large, I contain multitudes.)

I concentrate toward them that are nigh, I wait on the door-slab.

Who has done his day's work? who will soonest be through with his
   supper?
Who wishes to walk with me?

Will you speak before I am gone? will you prove already too late?
   (p. 74)

Finally, in part 52, the last section, he'll make his last prophecy,
dissolve himself into you the listener, the reader, and his poem
will become a part of your consciousness:

The spotted hawk swoops by and accuses me, he complains of my gab
   and my loitering.

I too am not a bit tamed, I too am untranslatable,
I sound my barbaric yawp over the roofs of the world.

The last scud of day holds back for me,
It flings my likeness after the rest and true as any on the shadow'd
   wilds,
It coaxes me to the vapor and the dusk.

I depart as air, I shake my white locks at the runaway sun,
I effuse my flesh in eddies, and drift it in lacy jags.

I bequeath myself to the dirt to grow from the grass I love,
if you want me again look for me under your boot-soles.
You will hardly know who I am or what I mean,
But I shall be good health to you nevertheless,

And filter and fibre your blood.

Failing to fetch me at first keep encouraged,
Missing me one place search another,
I stop somewhere waiting for you. (pp. 73–74)

That's a very deep, tearful promise: "I stop somewhere waiting for you." He's going to wait a long, long, long time, and have to go through a great deal of his own loves and fears before he actually finds a companion.

What kind of companion does he want, what does he look for? "The expression of the face balks account." This line is from the poem called "I Sing the Body Electric," in which he begins to describe his own body and other people's bodies in an intimate way, numbering all the parts, numbering the emotions, and naming them and actually attempting to give an accounting and itemization of all men. There is a little group of four or five lines where he describes what he's looking for:

The expression of the face balks account,
But the expression of a well-made man appears not only in his face.
It is in his limbs and joints also, it is curiously in the joints of his
    hips and wrists,
It is in his walk, the carriage of his neck, the flex of his waist and
    knees, dress does not hide him,
The strong sweet quality he has strikes through the cotton and
    broadcloth,
To see him pass conveys as much as the best poem, perhaps more,
You linger to see his back, and the back of his neck and shoulder-
    side. (pp. 77–78)

Well, everybody's done that, man or woman looking at who is interesting, who's got something going there. "Spontaneous me," he says, and so he keeps walking around, "has native moments."

In his short poem, "Native Moments," he defines what they are, when some authentic flash comes to him:

Native moments—when you come upon me—ah you are here now,
Give me libidinous joys only,
Give me the drench of my passions, give me life coarse and rank,
Today I go consort with Nature's darlings, to-night too,
I am for those who believe in loose delights, I share the midnight
    orgies of young men,

I dance with the dancers and drink with the drinkers,
The echoes ring with our indecent calls, I pick out some low person
  for my dearest friend,
He shall be lawless, rude, illiterate, he shall be one condemn'd by
  others for deeds done,
I will play a part no longer, why should I exile myself from my
  companions?
O you shunned persons, I at least do not shun you,
I come forthwith in your midst, I will be your poet,
I will be more to you than to any of the rest. (p. 91)

Here he is declaring his own feelings, he's not scared of them, as
if he were born for the first time in the world, recognizing his
own nature. The last poem in the first part of *Leaves of Grass* is
"As Adam Early in the Morning":

As Adam early in the morning,
Walking forth from the bower refresh'd with sleep,
Behold me where I pass, hear my voice, approach,
Touch me, touch the palm of your hand to my body as I pass,
Be not afraid of my body. (p. 92)

Well, there is some false note there I guess; he really wants
someone to love him, and he's not quite able to say it right. Still,
he does want to make democracy something that hangs together
using the force of Eros, as in "For You O Democracy," in the
"Calamus" section of *Leaves of Grass*:

Come, I will make the continent indissoluble,
I will make the most splendid race the sun ever shone upon,
I will make divine magnetic lands,
      With the love of comrades,
      With the life-long love of comrades.

I will plant companionship thick as trees along all the rivers of
  America, and along the shores of the great lakes, and all over the
  prairies,
I will make inseparable cities with their arms about each other's
  necks,
      By the love of comrades,
      By the manly love of comrades.

For you these from me, O Democracy, to serve you ma femme!
For you, for you I am trilling these songs. (p. 96)

That's Whitman's statement of his politics, but you never can tell, maybe he's just a big fairy egotist.

The "Calamus" section of *Leaves of Grass* describes erotic pleasure and parts of the body. When Whitman sent it to Ralph Waldo Emerson, it shocked the elder American prophet, who suggested that Whitman leave it out of the next edition of *Leaves of Grass*, because people were not ready for it. Whitman persisted, feeling that "Calamus" was an integral part of his message, that if he were going to talk about honesty and frankness and openness and comradeship he did have to say the unsayable, he did have to talk about people's bodies, he did have to describe them with beauty and Greek levity and healthiness and heroism. Nowadays "Calamus" seems very tame. However, he was a little worried:

I hear it was charged against me that I sought to destroy institu-
    tions,
But really I am neither for nor against institutions,
(What indeed have I in common with them? or what with the
    destruction of them?)
Only I will establish in the Mannahatta and in every city of these
    States inland and seaboard,
And in the fields and woods, and above every keel little or large that
    dents the water,
Without edifices or rules or trustees or any argument,
The institution of the dear love of comrades.

And that institution includes, like the prairie grass, everyone equal, so that there are "Those who look carelessly in the faces of Presidents and governors, as to say, *Who are you?*" (from "The Prairie-Grass Dividing").

So where's my big thrill like our big thrill nowadays?
Well, here's my big thrill, here's Whitman's big thrill:

A glimpse through an interstice caught,
Of a crowd of workmen and drivers in a bar-room around the stove
    late of a winter night, and I unremark'd seated in a corner,
Of a youth who loves me and whom I love, silently approaching and
    seating himself near, that he may hold me by the hand,
A long while amid the noises of coming and going, of drinking and
    oath and smutty jest,
Thus we two, content, happy in being together, speaking little,
    perhaps not a word. (p. 106)

So that's a recognizable emotion between friends.

But there may be things that he doesn't want to say even:

Earth, my likeness,
Though you look so impassive, ample and spheric there,
I now suspect that is not all;
I now suspect there is something fierce in you eligible to burst forth,
For an athlete is enamour'd of me, and I of him,
But toward him there is something fierce and terrible in me eligible
    to burst forth,
I dare not tell it in words, not even in these songs. (p. 107)

So there's more to come and it'll come out of Whitman as he goes forward in his life, renouncing all formulas.

His next long poem is called "Salut au Monde!" saying, "Come on, let's go out, let's explore life, let's find out what's going on here. Let's look at the tents of the Kalmucks and the Baskirs, let's go out and see the African and Asiatic towns, go to the Ganges, let's go to the groves of Mona where the Druids walked, and see the bodies of the gods, and wait at Liverpool and Glasgow and Dublin and Marseilles, wait at Valparaiso, Panama, sail on the waters of Hindustan, the China Sea, all the way around the world, on the road." So he begins: "Oh take my hand Walt Whitman! / Such gliding wonders!"—he's going to guide everybody on a trip around the world.

Then comes this very famous poem where he realizes, yeah, sure, but that's all transitory, it's going, there's not much, you know, like twenty years, fifty years, seventy years, then zap it's gone. So there is this great poem "Crossing Brooklyn Ferry" in which he realizes okay, he's had these feelings of being transitory, everybody has these kinds of feelings, but few have the chance to experience them deeply, much less say them aloud, much less propose them as politics, much less offer to save the nation with feelings, and at the same time even though it is very rare for people to understand all that, except that at the deepest moment of their lives, they *do* understand it. And, looking at the vast apparition of Manhattan and the masts of ships around it and the sunset and the sea gulls, he perceives the immensity of universe around him and the river on which he's riding and his own feelings and his ability to call these feelings out to people in the future. He says:

We understand then do we not?
What I promis'd without mentioning it, have you not accepted?
What the study could not teach—what the preaching could not
　accomplish is accomplish'd, is it not?

Flow on river! flow with the flood-tide, and ebb with the ebb-tide!
Frolic on, crested and scallop-edg'd waves!
Gorgeous clouds of the sunset! drench with your splendour me, or
　the men and women generations after me!
Cross from shore to shore, countless crowds of passengers!
Stand up, tall masts of Mannahatta! stand up, beautiful hills of
　Brooklyn!
Throb, baffled and curious brain! throw out questions and answers!
Suspend here and everywhere, eternal float of solution!
Gaze, loving and thirsting eyes, in the house or street or public
　assembly!
Sound out, voices of young men! loudly and musically call me by my
　nighest name!
Live, old life! play the part that looks back on the actor or actress!
Play the old role, the role that is great or small according as one
　makes it!
Consider, you who peruse me, whether I may not in unknown ways
　be looking upon you;
Be firm, rail over the river, to support those who lean idly, yet haste
　with the hasting current;
Fly on, sea-birds! fly sideways, or wheel in large circles high in the
　air;
Receive the summer sky, you water, and faithfully hold it till all
　downcast eyes have time to take it from you!
Diverge, fine spokes of light, from the shape of my head, or anyone's
　head, in the sunlit water! (pp. 131–132)

That's very subtle. You see, he gives you the sunshine halo,
aureole, aura around the hair reflected in the water. His noticing
is so exquisite and ethereal and fine that he's got the fine
centrifugal spokes of light round the shape of his head shining
in the water. The poem ends this way:

You have waited, you always wait, you dumb, beautiful ministers,
We receive you with free sense at last, and are insatiate
　henceforward,
Not you any more shall be able to foil us, or withhold yourselves
　from us,

We use you, and do not cast you aside—we plant you permanently
    within us,
We fathom you not—we love you—there is perfection in you also,
We furnish your parts towards eternity,
Great or small, you furnish your parts toward the soul. (pp. 132–133)

    After "Crossing Brooklyn Ferry" he needs someone to answer
him; his next long poem is "Song of the Answerer," in which he
imagines the answerer: what can be answered he answers, and
what cannot be answered he shows how it cannot be answered,
and he praises the words of true poems that do not merely please:

The true poets are not followers of beauty, but the august masters of
    beauty;
The greatness of sons is the exuding of the greatness of mothers and
    fathers,
The words of true poems are the tuft and final applause of science.

Divine instinct, breadth of vision, the law of reason, health, rudeness
    of body, withdrawnness,
Gayety, sun-tan, air-sweetness, such are some of the words of poems.
    (136)

    But there's a great tragedy coming up ahead. He's passed
through California and he's written about lonesome Kansas and
about birds of passage and a song of the rolling earth and the
ocean; then he's gone back to his birthplace in Long Island and
looked at the city, seeing a vision of birth continuous and death
continuous: again, sort of an ecstatic acknowledgment of the
continuity of feeling from generation to generation—like the
continuity of birth—that no matter what the appearances, there
always is a rebirth of delight, of feeling, of acknowledgment, of
the spaciousness of glittery sunlight on the ocean. Next come the
famous lines:

Out of the cradle endlessly rocking,
Out of the mocking-bird's throat, the musical shuttle,
Out of the Ninth-month midnight,
Over the sterile sands and the fields beyond, where the child leaving
    his bed wander'd alone, bareheaded, barefoot,
Down from the shower'd halo,
Up from the mystic play of shadows twining and twisting as if they
    were alive,

Out from the patches of briers and blackberries,
From the memories of the bird that chanted to me,
From your memories sad brother, from the fitful risings and fallings
 I heard,
From under that yellow half-moon late-risen and swollen as if with
 tears,
From those beginning notes of yearning and love there in the mist,
From the thousand responses of my heart never to cease,
From the myriad thence-aroused words,
From the word stronger and more delicious than any,
From such as now they start the scene revisiting,
As a flock, twittering, rising, or overhead passing,
Borne hither, ere all eludes me, hurriedly,
A man, yet by these tears a boy again,
Throwing myself on the sand, confronting the waves,
I, chanter of pains and joys, uniter of here and hereafter,
Taking all hints to use them, but swiftly leaping beyond them,
A reminiscence sing. (p. 198)

Of course the invocation here is classical: "Of Man's First
Disobedience and the Fruit/Of that Forbidden Tree, whose
mortal taste/Brought Death into the World, and all our woe. . .
Sing Heavenly Muse"—that's John Milton's opening of *Paradise
Lost*. Or the opening of Homer's *Iliad*: "Sing O Goddess of the
wrath of Achilles, Peleus's son, the ruinous wrath that brought
down countless woes upon the heads of the Achaeans and sent
many brave souls hurrying down to Hades and many a hero left
for prey to dogs and vultures . . ." or something like that. That
same long, long, long breath of realization that ends with a
trumpet call ("a reminiscence sing") leads to a reminiscence of a
whisper of death, when he was young at the ocean-side. Then, a
few prophecies of the presidents, and some patriotic songs, and
more awareness of the problems of America as it was going into
the Civil War.

   In the Civil War, Whitman, following his instincts, followed
the soldiers, went to Washington, did volunteer work in hospitals, took care of dying men, was out on the battlefields as a nurse
and saw Abe Lincoln on the streets numerous times. As Whitman was walking around on his own mission of mercy he wrote
a lot of poems, like "A Sight in Camp in the Daybreak Gray and
Dim"—this is a little snapshot, his same theme of human
diversity in the midst of the degradation of war:

A sight in camp in the daybreak gray and dim,
As from my tent I emerge so early sleepless,
As slow I walk in the cool fresh air the path near by the hospital
    tent,
Three forms I see on stretchers lying, brought out there untended
    lying,
Over each the blanket spread, ample brownish woolen blanket,
Gray and heavy blanket, folding, covering all.

Curious I halt and silent stand,
Then with light fingers I from the face of the nearest the first just
    lift the blanket;
Who are you elderly man so gaunt and grim, with well-gray'd hair,
    and flesh all sunken about the eyes?
Who are you my dear comrade?

Then to the second I step—and who are you my child and darling?
Who are you sweet boy with cheeks yet blooming?

Then to the third—a face nor child nor old, very calm, as of beautiful
    yellow-white ivory;
Young man I think I know you—I think this face is the face of the
    Christ himself,
Dead and divine and brother of all, and here again he lies. (p. 243)

He took care of the injured and the dying soldiers, and had
the same delicate emotional relationships:

O tan-faced prairie-boy,
Before you came to camp many a welcome gift,
Praises and presents came and nourishing food, till at last among
    the recruits,
You came, taciturn, with nothing to give—we but look'd on each
    other,
When lo! more than all the gifts of the world you gave me. (p. 253)

    Then, in the midst of the tragedies of the war and his visions
of death, there came the actual death of President Lincoln, and
so his great elegy for Lincoln, "When Lilacs Last in the Dooryard
Bloom'd," which most every kid in America knew back in the
twenties and thirties, with its very beautiful description of the
passing of Lincoln's coffin on railroad through lanes and streets,

through the cities and through the states and with processions, seas of silence, seas of faces and unbared heads, the coffin of Lincoln mourned, and in the middle of this poem a recognition of death in a way that had not been proposed in America before. Just as he had accepted the feelings of life, there was now the awareness of death that he had to tally finally. So there's this great italicized song in Part 14 of "When Lilacs Last in the Dooryard Bloom'd," from the section called "Memories of President Lincoln."

Actually, the whole of "When Lilacs Last in the Dooryard Bloom'd" is so beautiful that it would be worth reading here, but it's so long that I can't do it and also it's so beautiful that I'm afraid I'll cry if I read it. Read the most beautiful passages: Parts 1, 2, 3, 5, and 6, and go from there to the Hymn or Song to Death.

I visited Whitman's house in Camden, New Jersey, and in the back yard of the old brick house on Mickle Street, where he lived the last years of his life (though not where he wrote this poem), there were lilacs blooming in the back yard, blooming by the outhouse which was right outside the back door in the garden.

Then Whitman grew older, traveled, and extended his imagination to blue Ontario shore, and began to write about the declining of his own physical body in a series of poems called "Autumn Rivulets." He wrote about the compost ("This Compost"):

Behold this compost! behold it well!
Perhaps every mite has once form'd part of a sick person—yet
    behold!
The grass of spring covers the prairies,
The bean bursts noiselessly through the mould in the garden,
The delicate spear of the onion pierces upward. (p. 291)

After the carol to death there is the realization of the recycling of body and soul, the inevitability of passage, transitoriness, of things entering the earth and emerging from the earth. He wrote poems about the city dead-house too. These were all autumn rivulets, including his "Outlines for a Tomb."

Incidentally, he arranged for his own tomb at that point, made up a little drawing which he took from the opening page of William Blake's last great prophetic book *Jerusalem*, of a man entering an open door with stone pillars on each side, stone floor, stone arch, a triangular arch on top with a great stone door opened, a man carrying a great globe of light. A consciousness entering into this dark, he can't see what's in it, like passing through with a big black hat. This tomb is now standing in Camden, New Jersey, exactly like Blake's image. He wrote little poems to his own tomb then and to the negative and began to consider the negative: how do you recompost the negative?

•

He took a trip out to Kansas and wrote funny little poems about the burgeoning civilization that was beginning to cover the prairies. Here is a short poem, "The Prairie States":

A newer garden of creation, no primal solitude,
Dense, joyous, modern, populous millions, cities and farms,
With iron interlaced, composite, tied, many in one,
By all the world contributed—freedom's and law's and thrift's
     society,
The crowd and teeming paradise, so far, of time's accumulations,
To justify the past. (p. 315)

That was an ambitious and hopeful view; he might have changed his mind if he had seen Kansas during the Vietnam War, with its army bases and airplane bases and "iron interlaced" above the plains there, horrific iron.

Next he wrote a great poem that started to show a recognition of the Orient and the ancient wisdoms of death that were understood there—that is, the acceptance of death as well as the acceptance of life; he comes to see an identity between his own extended empathy and sympathy and compassion, and the ancient empathies and sympathies and compassions of the meditators of the Himalayas.

There's a very interesting section in "Passage to India." Remember, in the nineteenth century lots of poets and philosophers in America were interested in transcendentalism and oriental wisdom and Brahma and the Hindus and the romantic, glamorous wisdom of the East. There was also the Brook Farm experiment; Bronson Alcott and many other people were interested in Western gnosticism. Alcott went to England to buy up the neo-Platonic and hermetic translations of Thomas Taylor, the Platonist, translations from Greek Orphic and Dionysian mysteries, that were also read by the great British transcendental mystic poets like Coleridge, Shelley, and Blake—those same books were brought to Brook Farm and then these translations by Thomas Taylor of ancient hermetic Greek texts were circulated by Bronson Alcott to Emerson and to Thoreau and Hawthorne. So there existed this movement of transcendentalism and a recognition of the exotic East, along with the opening of Japan around that time. Lafcadio Hearn, maybe thirty years later, went to Japan and made great collections of Japanese art to bring to Boston to impress the New Englanders in the second wave of Oriental understanding, but in Europe, even at that time, Japanese prints by Hiroshige were circulating and were eyed by Gauguin and Van Gogh, who began imitating their flat surfaces and their bright colors. So, a whole new calligraphy of the mind was beginning to be discovered and absorbed by the West—at the same time that the West was peddling opium in China, oddly enough. That was the exchange, opium for meditation.

However, Whitman notes all these things in "Passage to India":

Lo soul, the retrospect brought forward,
The old, most populous, wealthiest of earth's lands,
The streams of the Indus and the Ganges and their many affluents,
(I my shores of America walking to-day behold, resuming all,)
The tale of Alexander on his warlike marches suddenly dying,
On one side China and on the other side Persia and Arabia,
To the south the great seas and the Bay of Bengal,
The flowing literatures, tremendous epics, religions, castes,
Old occult Brahma interminably far back, the tender and junior
   Buddha,
Central and southern empires and all their belongings, possessors,
The wars of Tamerlane, the reign of Aurungzebe,
The traders, rulers, explorers, Moslems, Venetians, Byzantium, the
   Arabs, Portuguese,
The first travelers famous yet, Marco Polo, Batouta the Moor,
Doubts to be solv'd, the map incognita, blanks to be fill'd,
The foot of man unstay'd, the hand never at rest,
Thyself O soul that will not brook a challenge. (p. 325)

He acknowledged that transcendent culture and, like D. H.

Lawrence fifty years later, wrote about that great ship of death that goes forward to explore:

O we can wait no longer,
We too take ship O soul,
Joyous we too launch out on trackless seas,
Fearless for unknown shores on waves of ecstasy to sail
Amid the wafting winds, (thou pressing me to thee, I thee to me, O
    soul,)
Caroling free, singing our song of God,
Chanting our chant of pleasant exploration. (p. 326)

He's talking about going through the soul as well as going through the world.

However, most of the world is asleep, alas. His long poem "The Sleepers" was written earlier, before 1855, but he moved it into his poems of middle age. Death is coming a bit into his mind as he gets into his fifties and sixties. To him it appears that most of the people living in the world are the living dead or the sleepers:

I wander all night in my vision,
Stepping with light feet, swiftly and noiselessly stepping and
    stopping,
Bending with open eyes over the shut eyes of sleepers,
Wandering and confused, lost to myself, ill-assorted, contradictory,
Pausing, gazing, bending and stopping.

How solemn they look there, stretch'd and still,
How quiet they breathe, the little children in their cradles.

The wretched features of ennuyés, the white features of corpses, the
    livid faces of drunkards, the sick-gray faces of onanists,
The gash'd bodies on battle-fields, the insane in their strong-door'd
    rooms, the sacred idiots, the new-born emerging from gates, and
    the dying emerging from gates,
The night pervades them and infolds them.

The married couple sleep calmly in their bed, he with his palm on
    the hip of the wife, and she with her palm on the hip of the
    husband,
The sisters sleep lovingly side by side in theirs,
The men sleep lovingly side by side in theirs,
And the mother sleeps with her little child carefully wrapt.

The blind sleep, and the deaf and dumb sleep,
The prisoner sleeps well in the prison, the runaway son sleeps,
The murderer that is to be hung next day, how does he sleep?
And the murder'd person, how does he sleep? (p. 331)

All are sleepers, he says at the end of the poem, and begins to think of the future, what'll happen to him:

I too pass from the night,
I stay a while away O night, but I return to you again and love you.

Why should I be afraid to trust myself to you?
I am not afraid, I have been well brought forward by you,
I love the rich running day, but I do not desert her in whom I lay so
    long,
I know not how I came of you and I know not where I go with you,
    but I know I came well and shall go well.

I will stop only a time with the night, and rise betimes,
I will duly pass the day O my mother, and duly return to you.
    (p. 338)

The next section in *Leaves of Grass* is called "Whispers of Heavenly Death." Its poems are very interesting, beginning to get closer and closer to the grand subject of all poetry. "Quicksand Years" is a very charming little statement on that. Now he's beginning to doubt himself a little:

Quicksand years that whirl me I know not whither,
Your schemes, politics fail, lines give way, substances mock and
    elude me,
Only the theme I sing, the great and strong-possess'd soul, eludes
    not,
One's-self must never give way—that is the final substance—that
    out of all is sure,
Out of politics, triumphs, battles, life, what at last finally remains?
When shows break up what but One's-Self is sure? (p. 350)

How does he know that? Well, he's going to get older; we'll see what happens next.

This is an interesting thing, because now he realizes that it is the notion of an unconquerable self or soul that all along has sustained him, but that too, will dissolve and he's going to let it dissolve. He has a few thoughts about the dissolution, also, incidentally, just as of his soul, of the soul of the nation, the dissolution of democracy, and in those days, of public opinion. His poem "Thoughts" makes you think of Watergate:

Of public opinion,
Of a calm and cool fiat sooner or later, (how impassive! how certain
  and final!)
Of the President with pale face asking secretly to himself, *What will
  the people say at last?*

and it foreshadows Bob Dylan's "Even the President of the United States someday must stand naked."

"So long!" finally he says. "So Long" I think of as the last great poem of *Leaves of Grass*, a salutation and farewell and summary, conclusion, triumph, disillusion, giving up, taking it all on, giving it all over to you who are listening. "So Long!":

To conclude, I announce what comes after me.

I remember I said before my leaves sprang at all,
I would raise my voice jocund and strong with reference to consum-
  mations.

When America does what is promis'd,
When through these States walk a hundred millions of superb
  persons,
When the rest part away for superb persons and contribute to them,
When breeds of the most perfect mothers denote America,
Then to me and mine our due fruition.

I have press'd through in my own right,
I have sung the body and soul, war and peace have I sung, and the
  songs of life and death,
And the songs of birth and shown that there are many births.

I have offer'd my style to every one, I have journey'd with confident
  step;
While my pleasure is yet at the full I whisper *So long!*
And take the young woman's hand and the young man's hand for the
  last time.
[. . .]

Dear friend whoever you are take this kiss,
I give it especially to you, do not forget me,
I feel like one who has done work for the day to retire awhile,
I receive now again of my many translations, from my avataras
    ascending, while others doubtless await me,
An unknown sphere more real than I dream'd, more direct, darts
    awakening rays about me, *So long!*
Remember my words, I may again return,
I love you, I depart from materials,
I am as one disembodied, triumphant, dead. (pp. 389–392)

But he wasn't dead yet, he was only seventy. He's still got to go through the actual dying, how does he do that? How does he take that? What has he got to say about that? There are some interesting "Sands at Seventy" thoughts about giving out—he was quite ill and old in his seventies—in the sense of old in body—his gallstones, paralysis, uremia probably, emphysema, and the great many of his heart difficulties. The poet Jonathan Williams noted that his autopsy showed him to have been as "universal" in his illnesses near death as he was universal in his healths in life. He wrote little poems, then, just whatever he could write now, his great major work over, and yet the little trickle-drops of wisdom of a man of seventy are exquisite and curious:

As I sit writing here, sick and grown old,
Not my least burden is that dullness of the years, querilities,
Ungracious glooms, aches, lethargy, constipation, whimpering *ennui*,
May filter in my daily songs. (p. 394)

And he's got a little poem to his canary bird: he's stuck in his little upstairs bedroom in Camden, on Mickle Street, in a little house with low ceilings, visited by many people and talking to his canary bird:

Did we count great, O soul, to penetrate the themes of mighty books,
Absorbing deep and full from thoughts, plays, speculations?
But now from thee to me, caged bird, to feel thy joyous warble,
Filling the air, the lonesome room, the long forenoon,
Is it not just as great, O soul? (395)

Then, "Queries to My Seventieth Year":

Approaching, nearing, curious,
Thou dim, uncertain spectre—bringst thou life or death?
Strength, weakness, blindness, more paralysis and heavier?
Or placid skies and sun? Wilt stir the waters yet?
Or haply cut me short for good? Or leave me here as now,
Dull, parrot-like and old, with crack'd voice harping, screeching? (p.
  395)

Well, everything wasn't all bad, he had his first dandelion,
springtime:

Simple and fresh and fair from winter's close emerging,
As if no artifice of fashion, business, politics, had ever been,
Forth from its sunny nook of shelter'd grass—innocent, golden, calm
  as the dawn,
The spring's first dandelion shows its trustful face. (p. 395)

He still had his same witty awareness, even lying in his sickbed.
    Then people began exploring the North Pole, and this amazes
him:

Of that blithe throat of thine from arctic bleak and blank,
I'd mind the lesson, solitary bird—let me too welcome chilling drifts,
E'en the profoundest chill, as now—a torpid pulse, a brain unnerv'd,
Old age landlock'd within its winter bay—(cold, cold, O cold!)
These snowy hairs, my feeble arm, my frozen feet,
For them thy faith, thy rule I take, and grave it to the last;
Not summer's zones alone—nor chants of youth, or south's warm
  tides alone,
But held by sluggish floes, pack'd in the northern ice, the cumulus of
  years,
These with gay heart I also sing. (p. 402)

He's no longer dependent on that youthful self, in fact the self is
dissolving, as it will in these last poems—that's what wisdom
brings. In "To Get the Final Lilt of Songs," he says:

To get the final lilt of songs,
To penetrate the inmost lore of poets—to know the mighty ones,
Job, Homer, Eschylus, Dante, Shakspere, Tennyson, Emerson;
To diagnose the shifting-delicate tints of love and pride and doubt—
  to truly understand,
To encompass these, the last keen faculty and entrance-price,

31

Old age and what it brings from all its past experiences. (p. 403)

You need that, otherwise you ain't gonna learn nuttin' if you don't grow old and die, you just know what you have in your mind when you think you've got the world by the crotch.

Next comes an odd lament for the aborigines, an Iroquois term *Yonnondio*, the sense of the word is "lament for the aborigines." It turns into an odd little political poem at the end, warning us of Black Mesa, of the Four Corners, of the civilization's destruction of the land and its original natives. He's also saying that as he dies, so may all the machinery of the civilization, so there's nothing for anybody to get too high and mighty about.

But he's got to give thanks in old age, in a poem of that title:

Thanks in old age—thanks ere I go,
For health, the midday sun, the impalpable air—for life, mere life,
For precious ever-lingering memories, (of you my mother dear—you,
    father—you brothers, sisters, friends,)
For all my days—not those of peace alone—the days of war the same,
For gentle words, caresses, gifts from foreign lands,
For shelter, wine and meat—for sweet appreciation,
(You distant, dim unknown—or young or old—countless, unspecified,
    readers belov'd,
We never met, and ne'er shall meet—and yet our souls embrace,
    long, close and long;)
For beings, groups, love, deeds, words, books—for colors, forms,
For all the brave strong men—devoted, hardy men—who've forward
    sprung in freedom's help, all years, all lands,
For braver, stronger, more devoted men—(a special laurel ere I go, to
    life's war's chosen ones,
The cannoneers of song and thought—the great artillerists—the
    foremost leaders, captains of the soul:)
As soldier from an ended war return'd—As traveler out of myriads,
    to the long procession retrospective,
Thanks—joyful thanks!—a soldier's, traveler's thanks.

But there is also "Stronger Lessons"—is everything thanks for the memories and thanks for the good times, and thanks for the gifts and thanks for the loves? "Stronger Lessons":

Have you learn'd lessons only of those who admired you, and were
    tender with you, and stood aside for you?

Have you not learned great lessons from those who reject you, and
  brace themselves against you? or who treat you with contempt, or
  dispute the passage with you?

That's a good piece of advice on how to alchemize fear to bliss,
how to alchemize contrariety to harmony, how to roll with the
punches, so to speak. But what is it all about? So he's got, finally,
twilight, not quite sure about that old self. "Twilight":

The soft voluptuous opiate shades,
The sun just gone, the eager light dispell'd—(I too soon will be gone,
  dispell'd,)
A haze—nirwana—rest and night—oblivion.

But there are still a few thoughts left in his mind before he
goes off into that rest and night: "You Lingering Sparse Leaves
of Me" and "Now Precedent Songs, Farewell." Then, having
sum-med up his life, well, just waiting around, "An Evening
Lull":

After a week of physical anguish,
Unrest and pain, and feverish heat,
Toward the ending day a calm and lull comes on,
Three hours of peace and soothing rest of brain.

Then, "After the Supper and Talk" is the last of the poems in
"Sands at Seventy," and perhaps his last. But that wasn't his last
word, no, because he lived on. There are also "Good-Bye My
Fancy," "Second Annex," and "Preface Note to the Second Annex,"
where he says:

Reader, you must allow a little fun here—for one reason there are
too many of the following poemets about death, &c., and for another
the passing hours (July 5, 1890) are so sunny-fine. And old as I am
I feel to-day almost a part of some frolicsome wave, or for sporting
yet like a kid or kitten— . . .

Still there are a couple of little last poems, such as "My 71st
Year" and "Long, Long Hence":

After a long, long course, hundreds of years, denials,
Accumulations, rous'd love and joy and thought,
Hopes, wishes, aspirations, ponderings, victories, myriads of readers,

Coating, compassing, covering—after ages' and ages' encrustations,
Then only may these songs reach fruition.

Well, that's actually what happened to him, in the sense that his work was little famous, not much read, and a bit put down in the first years after his death.

Still clinging on, Whitman recognizes what it was that was his victory: the commonplace, ordinary mind, as it is known around the world.

The commonplace I sing:
How cheap is health! how cheap nobility!
Abstinence, no falsehood, no gluttony, lust;
The open air I sing, freedom, toleration,
(Take here the mainest lesson—less from books—less from the
     schools,)
The common day and night—the common earth and waters,
Your farm—your work, trade, occupation,
The democratic wisdom underneath, like solid ground for all. (p. 426)

He knows the basis, where everybody could stand, which is where we all actually are, and is recognizable in our own bodies, in our own thoughts, in our own work, in our own nation, in our own local particulars—a wisdom that was inherited by Ezra Pound and William Carlos Williams and whole generations of poets after Walt Whitman who had discovered that common ground of self and dissolution of self, common ground of his own mind and the common ground of city pavement he walked on with his fellow citizens and the common ground of their emotions between them.

Finally he can with good conscience say farewell to his part, to his own fancy, to his own imagination, to his own life's work, to his own life, in "Good-Bye My Fancy":

Good-bye my Fancy!
Farewell dear mate, dear love!
I'm going away, I know not where,
Or to what fortune, or whether I may ever see you again,
So Good-bye my Fancy.

Now for my last—let me look back a moment;
The slower, fainter ticking of the clock is in me,

Exit, nightfall, and soon the heart-thud stopping.

Long have we lived, joy'd, caress'd together;
Delightful—now separation—Good-bye my Fancy.

Yet let me not be too hasty,
Long indeed have we lived, slept, filter'd, become really blended into
    one;
Then if we die we die together, (yes, we'll remain one,)
If we go anywhere we'll go together to meet what happens,
May-be we'll be better off and blither, and learn something,
May-be it is yourself now really ushering me to the true songs, (who
    knows?)
May-be it is you the mortal knob really undoing, turning—so now
    finally,
Good-bye—and hail! my Fancy! (p. 429)

And that's counted as almost his last poem, but then he didn't
die, he had to go on, poor fellow, thinking, allowing his executor
to arrange *Old Age Echoes*, an appendix to *Leaves of Grass*, which
ends with "A Thought of Columbus," a forward-looking poem
about exploration, navigation, going on into worlds unknown,
unconquered, etc. "A Thought of Columbus" is not his most
moving poem, or his greatest poem, but on the other hand is the
last poem he wrote (December 1891) and contains maybe his
last thoughts.

So, his life ended on a heroical historical note, congratulating
the explorer, himself really, or the Columbus in himself, and the
Columbus in all of us seeking outward in our spiritual journey
looking not even for truth, because it wasn't truth he was
proposing, except the truth of the fact that we are here with our
lusts and delights, our givings-up and our grabbings, growing
into trouble and marriage and birth and growing into coffins and
earth and unbirth. Good character, all in all, the kind of character that if a nation were composed of such liberal, large-
minded gentlemen of the old school or young, large-bodied
persons with free emotions and funny thoughts and tender
looks, there might be a possibility of this nation and other
nations surviving on the planet, but to survive, we'd have to take
on some of that large magnanimity that Whitman yawped over
the rooftops of the world.

Whitman's Words

by Kenneth Koch

I celebrate myself
And what I shall assume you shall assume
For every atom belonging to me as good belongs to you.

I loafe and invite my soul
I lean and loafe at my ease . . . observing a spear of summer grass.

If you put the thoughts expressed in these opening lines of "Song of Myself" into ordinary speech, they are rather flat and uninteresting:

I myself am what I am celebrating; and everything that I am, you
   are also, since you and I are both made out of the same materials.
   I'm really taking it easy, lying around and communing with my
   soul, while I look at a blade of grass.

Whitman's lines don't rhyme and they have no regular meter. There must be other things about them that make them so interesting and suggestive and exciting to read. These things, of course, are the words and the ways Whitman puts them together. By looking closely at these words and uses, one may be able to get closer to the mystery of poetry, of Whitman's in any case, and to be inspired by "Song of Myself" and to write like it and to understand it. I ask my students to pick out words and phrases they wouldn't be likely to hear in conversation or to read in an essay or newspaper article. What's peculiar about the way Whitman is talking? My college students find most of the oddities in the lines; and, with a bit more help, I think younger students could also:

1) Nobody ever says "I celebrate"; instead one says "I'm celebrating." "I celebrate" sounds like someone making a speech on a formal occasion: "Today we celebrate the birthday of a great American."

2) *Myself* would never come after *celebrate* in normal talk or prose writing. What one celebrates is a birthday, a holiday, a wedding, a victory. Celebrating oneself seems crazy.

3) Repeating a word as Whitman repeats the word *assume* in line 2 with just two words between—what I *assume* you shall *assume*—draws attention to the sound of the word in a way that's not usual in talking or prose-writing. *Assume*, the second time it's used, is as much music as it is meaning.

4) It's not completely clear what Whitman means by *assume*. In fact, the word seems either to be used wrongly or to mean two things at once. *Assume* can mean "take for granted" or it can mean "take or put on"—you can assume the role of king, and you can assume that it's nighttime, because it's dark. In conversation, or in an article, the writer would have to be clearer and to choose one of these meanings or the other. In poetry, having two meanings at once can be an advantage—it can make what you say suggestive, mysterious, true in some way it couldn't otherwise be.

5) The word *atom* is a scientific word that doesn't belong with words like *celebrate* and *assume*. It's unexpected and a little jarring—as would be, say, the word *oxygen* in the statement, "Come, let us walk through the oxygen."

6) The repetition of *belong*, like the earlier repetition of *assume*, puts an emphasis on sounds that isn't usual in speech or expository prose.

7) In the phrase "as good belongs to you," "as good" is a very folksy, plain expression, not at all what you'd expect in a discourse about atoms, and just as surprising after *atom* as *atom* was after *celebrate* and *assume*. (Another example of folksiness and science might be "This is mighty fine radium.")

8) There's a little rhyming in "assume . . . assume" and "you" (in line 2 and then another "you" in line 3) that probably wouldn't happen in talking or plain prose. Like word repetition, sound repetition (rhyme is one kind) draws attention to the physical qualities of words and gives them music along with their meanings.

9) The idea of *loafing* seems a big jump from the philosophical speculations on identity that precede it. Such an apparent jump in subject matter might make prose or conversation hard to follow. In poetry it can be exciting. In poetry, when there's a jump, you just jump, and afterwards you see where you are.

10) The lowly, folksy word *loafe* (an older spelling of *loaf*) seems out of place in the same sentence with *soul*, which is a very "high-class," serious word.

11) There's a partial rhyme in the words *loafe* and *soul*, which would tend to make one keep the two words farther apart in talk or in prose.

12) Repeating *loafe* the way Whitman does in lines 4 and 5 would be needlessly repetitious in prose.

13) The expression "at my ease" would seem repetitious and maybe even stupid in prose, since how else would you "loafe"— tensely? painfully? vigorously?

14) The word *observing* seems too serious and official for looking at a grass blade. Astronomers observe planets and detectives observe criminals, but why observe a plain old blade of grass?

15) *Spear* is a strange word for grass—the usual word is *blade* (which was doubtless strange when it was first used).

16) Like the repetitions and the rhymes in other lines, all the *s* sounds in the last half line draw attention to the physical qualities of the words and make some music.

17) Throughout the passage the present tense is used in a way that would certainly be strange in an article or conversation—as if one were to say, "I turn on the light, I go to the door and take you in my arms." Who talks that way?

To sum up, one finds in Whitman's lines a mixture of plain and fancy (including religious and scientific and colloquial) words, repetitions of words and sounds that tend to partly change the words into music, vagueness, seemingly "wrong" uses of words, odd combinations of words, jumps in subject matter, and an odd present tense. These oddnesses and "mistakes" make his lines different from prose and are part of what makes them poetry.

Reading such strangely mixed language so full of leaps and other surprises is not like reading the newspaper. It gives a different kind of meaning and does it in a different way.

Seeing the peculiarities of Whitman's language can help students to enjoy writing like Whitman as well as to understand "Song of Myself." A good writing exercise for students is to ask them to write four or five lines using as many of Whitman's oddities as they can; for example, to start with a phrase like "I celebrate" (or "I prophesy," "I command," "I entertain") and to follow that with something as unlikely as *myself* (Wednesday morning, ice-cold drinks, my dog, sleeping). Then maybe a line with a word repeated like *assume* (And what I endorse you shall endorse) and so on. They are likely to have a good time doing this—it's silly-seeming but inspiring. It leads to something—for one thing, an enlarged sense of what can be done with language, if you try strange things with it, especially in poems.

Of course the sense of the opening lines, and of the rest of "Song of Myself," is closely connected to all that seems odd in the words. For example, for Whitman it makes perfect sense to announce a formal celebration of himself. A person's ordinary self is more wonderful than any special particular day or event. And the best way to celebrate the self is just to lie around and take it easy, to loaf and look at things. And a grass blade is exactly the kind of thing that's worthy of being observed: it's plain, it's common, it's alive, it's eternally reborn, it's fresh and green, it proves there is no death. What better thing to look at? No monument can compare to it. And if loafing is the right way to behave, you get a better sense of it from saying it slowly, from repeating—"I loafe" and "I lean and loafe at my ease." *Atom* is a fine word to use because scientific and literary and plain words are all equal and all part of the divine oneness and variety that Whitman finds in everything: words, people, animals, places. There are no privileged characters in Whitman and no privileged words. And so "as good belongs to you," folksy though it is, is just fine for a philosophical statement. What's easiest and most natural is what's truest; profundity's in plain talk and not in fancy academic or poetical speech. As for the present tense, it is perfect for saying "This is always going on, it's always true, it's always wonderful, it's always right here and right now."

Finally, what Whitman has to say about the oneness of all things is quite mysterious. It can't be logically proven, can't be rationally shown. But rhymes, repetitions, and even vagueness can help us to feel it. There is an exciting dreamy convincingness in "what I assume you shall assume" that would be lacking, for example, in a phrase such as "we're just alike." Once you see, and help others to see, the connections between the (not really separate) language and meaning of "Song of Myself," reading this long, complicated-seeming poem should be easier, and, as Whitman might say, luckier.

Whitman's Long Lines

by Jim Berger

Open Whitman's *Leaves of Grass*. Some of the poems are short, others long, but they *all* have long lines.

Long lines are oceanic. They wash over you like waves, one after another, each of them full of shells and sand and fish and surfboards, sometimes pieces of wrecks and the bodies of sailors. The long line is more conclusive and inclusive than the partial, subdivided short line. If short lines are like quick pants, long lines resemble great, deep breaths.

That's how I present long lines to students at first, as units of breath. I tell them, "Take a deep breath, then as you exhale, make up your line. When you take a new breath, start a new line." Sometimes the long line will resemble a long sentence; other times it will look like a short paragraph. I try to demonstrate extemporaneously: I take a dramatic deep breath, then try to exhale some words that sound like poetry: "Outside it's raining and I suspect that the roof is leaking. Oh no! It's falling on that boy's head! Quick, get a towel!" I show by my voice and gesture that I've run out of breath, so I take a great new breath and resume. "There, that's better. Lightning and thunder! The chalkboard is a cradle for a whale and all the different pairs of shoes have lost their feet and are smearing the desks with mud." It's just an example to demonstrate the procedure.

Then I have the students make up a few of their own and write them down, since they may be too shy to compose them spontaneously out loud. But I do want them to read the lines aloud. I make it a kind of game to see who can make up the longest line that can be read in a single breath.

Sometimes students need to be shown how to arrange long lines on the page. Since each line of the poem will very likely go beyond the physical line of the paper, the student should continue his or her poetic line on the next physical line by leaving a small indentation. This will show that it's still the same line being continued. The next new poetic line will begin at the margin again. It helps to illustrate this on the chalkboard.

Teaching long-line poems doesn't require the detailed examination of the form that teaching short-line poems does, at least at the introductory level. Writing a poem with long lines takes a bit more patience and endurance, and requires more than just the inspiration to crystalize an instant: the writer has to have something to write about. So what I stress in long-line poems—after the breath unit—is the subject matter or genre. The two broad types that seem to fit best with long-line poems are the narrative and the catalog.

Whitman gave the catalog poem its modern cast. The catalog poem is basically a list—but a list with personality, with life. One type of catalog poem focuses on a particular object—a friend, a car, an animal, for instance—and tells everything the poet knows, sees, feels about that thing. One of the great poems of this sort is Christopher Smart's "Jubilate Agno," which shows wonderful perceptiveness and love for his cat Jeoffrey, but then expands from the details of his cat's life to a sense of God's presence in the world. Here is a short excerpt:

For he will not do destruction if he is well fed, neither will he spit without provocation.
For he purrs in thankfulness, when God tells him he's a good cat.
For he is an instrument for the children to learn benevolence upon.
For every house is incompleat without him & a blessing is lacking in the spirit.
For the Lord commanded Moses concerning the cats at the departure of the Children of Israel from Egypt.
For every family had one cat at least in the bag.
For the English cats are the best in Europe.

For younger kids the language of Smart's poem is hard, but you can probably find a short passage that will make the point. Other good catalog poems are African praise poems. This is a good type of poem to do as a group, in which each student can contribute a line. Also, when each student contributes a line (or two or three), you don't have to deal with writer's cramp, a problem with younger students writing at length in a single sitting.

Another possibility of the catalog poem is to be more universal and list lots of things. Whitman's "Song of Myself" is a good example. His narrator is a kind of supernatural being who sees everything, both outside and inside—"tenacious, acquisitive, tireless . . . and can never be shaken away." His powers of observation are infinite, and so is his power of sympathy. He not only sees, but emotionally enters what he sees.

For younger students, just a few lines from *Leaves of Grass*, preferably written on the board, will serve as an example. Older students can digest a longer excerpt. Here are some lines from section 8 of "Song of Myself":

The little one sleeps in its cradle,
I lift the gauze and look a long time, and silently brush away flies with
   my hand.

The youngster and the redfaced girl turn aside up the bushy hill,
I peeringly view them from the top.

The suicide sprawls on the bloody floor of the bedroom,
It is so . . . . I witnessed the corpse . . . . there the pistol had fallen.

And so on. With older students, I recommend that you go over the entire passage. You can point out the variety and contrast in the things Whitman sees, and how he moves so quickly among them, like a movie camera or a ghost; how he tried to include a whole society in his poem, just giving a line or two for each thing, but how there's action in every line; and how he makes you see and hear every event. He says something particular about each thing. The expansiveness of his vision is beautifully offset by the minuteness of his details.

Here are two examples of student work:

Animals

Birds—free and spiritual, swooping down, going to the bathroom on
   your head.
Or a camel—slow and spitting on the ground; ignorant and lazy, an
   annoying movement.
Cats—constantly meowing and purring; graceful and with poise—they
   move like ballerinas.
These tigers seem to be laughing at you—Ha Ha—I may eat you up—
   They're truly crazy!
I love the giraffe—he's kind of towering over us—keeping an eye on the
   trees.

Oh, God, not the cow! What a pitiful sound—Moooooooo! Can't you think
    of anything better to say?
I think I'm paranoid! Ticks! Ticks! Ticks!
Don't come near me! I hate you!
What a cunning animal—that kangaroo! So close to its baby—always
    hopping around. Doesn't it ever get tired? Not like that
Rhinoceros—fat and slobbering—dragging its huge putrid body from
    place to place.
Ah! The adorable little prairie dog—I'm sure all little children would
    love to have one.
Don't fly away! You idiotic pigeon—can't you see that I'm going to feed
    you?
You darling monkey! How do you swing on the trees so easily? Your body
    seems to be made of rubber bands.
You sweet puppy! Flopping ears and wet nose—so loyal and faithful you
    are!
Ooh! What a gory feline—this flesh-eating, prey-stalking panther—a
    regular threat to the human race!
And Fish! How innocent and gentle you are! Swimming around lazily all
    day . . . .
      —*Nicole, age 12*

Annoying People

Annoying people comb their hair when it already looks good.
They drive their cars with jerks and short stops and purposely avoid
    bumps.
They go around singing off-key.
They crack their gum during tests.
They always have ink marks on their faces.
Annoying people wear the wrong color lipstick.
They play louder than anyone else in the orchestra and play the wrong
    notes.
They complain all the time and their sneakers stay perfectly white for
    about two years.
Their clothes never match and their clothes always match.
Annoying people wear too much perfume and don't shave their legs.
They talk too much in class and suck up to teachers.
They always get high grades on tests and they say that it's not very good.
Annoying people's glasses always fall to the tip of their noses and they
    don't push them back up.
They waddle when they walk and they never mind their own business.
They wear too much blush.

Annoying people pretend they know how to smoke and don't inhale.
They button up their shirts to the top and then put up their collars. They
wear bell bottoms and high heels.
Annoying people swim badly and recite TV commercials.
They stretch out the elastic in their socks.
Annoying people leave a light on when they go to sleep and call during
dinner all the time.
Annoying people don't really know their ass from their elbow about a
certain subject and then try and tell you what to do.
They speak slowly and whine.
Annoying people tell really bad jokes and then laugh at them . . . alone.
        —*Samantha, age 15*

Teaching "Song of Myself" to Children

by Kenneth Koch

Song of Myself" (sections 1 and 2) is appealing to children because it offers them secret knowledge and power in a fresh, friendly, breezy, almost Santa-Clausy kind of way. Whitman says "I'm terrific, and you're terrific too. Come along with me and we'll see and do great things!" His tone is a combination of boasting and open-hearted generosity—"I know it all, and I'm going to share it with you!" And that Whitman says that his kind of secret knowledge is better than what is found in books is of course refreshing to children reading it in school. Children can identify rather easily with Whitman's claim to have important secret knowledge: they know things that are obviously important, that adults apparently don't know (though Whitman seems to)—how to be close to animals and other creatures and to nature, how beautiful the world is, and how exciting and endless it is to be alive in it.

As a poetry idea I told the children to suppose that they knew secrets that gave them a special power and to write a poem in which, in a boasting, generous, and secret-telling kind of way, they offer to share these secrets. I gave and asked for examples of some kinds of things people could know—what it is like under the ocean, why the sky is blue, what the rain hears, what the grass and stones say. But secrets are secrets, and I told the children to keep the best secrets for themselves and for their poems.

They wrote about secret knowledge and special powers of many kinds. The reader is invited to the other side of the moon, to the world of secrets, to the inside of a flower, "up the path to nowhere," into dreams, and to a "world of our own to live the way we want." He is offered knowledge of how things really are beneath surface appearances, of where to find out about things, of the origins of things, of the history of the world, of the nature of happiness, of the reason for human cruelty, and of how it feels to be hurt. Some poems were mainly about superhero powers; others, like Vivien's and Marion's, about escaping into a place

45

free of restrictions and cares. The familiar childhood idea of a "special secret place" where certain things can be seen appears in quite a few of the poems.

A Whitman-like use of the repetition and rhetoric of speech-making appears in some of the children's poems. A few children picked up Whitman's "plain-talking" and sometimes rather "smart-alecky" tone, too—"This is not a side show, don't be mistaken . . ." (Tracy); "Do you know how to get to the end of the universe? I do. If you don't, you won't find it in the almanac . . ." (Lisa).

There are other sections of "Song of Myself" that would be as good to teach as these—in section 15, for example, the great list beginning "The pure contralto," or section 26 about the sounds the poet hears. Parts of these sections could be read to children along with sections 1 and 2 to give them more ideas. Whichever part of the poem a teacher chooses, I would suggest it be one that is suffused with Whitman's big breezy sensuousness, secrecy, and power, for I think that is the quality of his poetry that speaks to children most. I would suggest not teaching the frequently used "What Is Grass" episode in section 6 of the poem, which, if taken by itself, lacks this quality.

Poems by Sixth Graders

What I Know

Come with me to the other side of the moon.
I'll tell you where the moon comes from.
And where we come from
Where the sky came from
Come with me
This is not a side show, don't be mistaken
I can open the world with my brain, and yours can do it too. COME
   WITH ME. . . .
      —*Tracy Lahab*

A Flower to Go To

Come with me to a flower.
I know I can get there and it's a beautiful place.
It's the insides of a flower—it's beautiful especially if you and I are
    going to share it.
We'll go there tonight at twilight, we'll meet there when the sky is
    orange and the moon is pink. We'll go in
And ask one another questions and love this secret place of love.
    —*Vivien Tuft*

Come with Me

Come with me and I'll show you my heart. I know where it is. I know
    all about it.
Come with me to a place I know. It's a very mysterious place. I get
    there through the back roads of my mind.
Come with me, I'll take you to a world, not a world that you know.
    Not a world that nobody knows, not me or you. It's a world of our
    own to live the way we want.
To do the things we want.
To know the things we want.
There's no way to get there.
It's ourselves that takes us there.
    —*Vivien Tuft*

Come with me to the world of secrets.
Do you know how a mind grows? I do. Do you? If you don't, you won't
    find it on a piece of paper, you'll find it on the dark blue sky.
Do you know how to get to the end of the universe? I do. If you don't,
    you won't find it in the almanac, you'll find it in the number nine.
Do you know where fish came from? I do. If you don't, you won't find
    it in a book about fish, you'll find it on the earth's equator.
    —*Lisa Smalley*

Fish

Do you know what—I'm half fish and half man
I look normal
But once I'm in the water
I turn gold
I turn and toss and talk to the fish

47

Why? I guess it's because I love the chilly blue green water
It's so silky
Once I get out I'm me again
I wish I was a fish all the time
No cares, no troubles, free of everything
Everything on earth.
  —Marion Mackles

Come with me to my world of secrets.
One of my secrets is when the sun is shining on Manhattan, it's
 really a glittering star of darkness.
One of my secrets is when the stars are sparkling in the night, it is
 really a moon of brightness.
One of my secrets is that a little fly is really an enormous butterfly
 in feelings.
  —Jeannie Turner

Come with Me . . .

Come with me and I'll show you a rabbit with no head.
Come with me on a mountain and I'll show you a live skeleton.
Come with me and I'll show you one million nothings.
  —Lorraine Fedison

Sunny Day

Come with me, I'll show a secret. The sun shines when I feel good,
 and if I don't, it will become breezy.
  —Hipolito Rivera

Breezy, Breezy

Oh Breezy, Breezy, I'll show a secret to you. I am lucky, knuckle-
 headed.
  —Hipolito Rivera

The sky is filled with flying mermaids which are invisible to every-
 one but me.
But when you go underwater, all you can see is scuba-diving devils.
  —Billy Constant

One day, a nice warm day, I took a long swim in a pool of water. I heard a voice! Whose voice could it be? Then I looked up. I saw the moon's face. I looked at it. I saw the mouth of the moon say something and in a few minutes I had a shock in the water. I could not understand the moon's language, and in one minute I understood it—fantastic! I talked with the moon all night. Then I went to bed. In the morning I went to my friend's house. I told him to come and I would teach him to talk with the moon too. So then night came again. I went out to take a swim. When the voice appeared I told my friend I would teach him to talk with the moon, and in a few minutes my friend talked with the moon. He could not believe his ears, but I taught him to speak moon language. I made money teaching people to talk moon.

—*Miklos Lengyel*

Close your eyes and follow me to the secret cave full of thought.
Only your thinking will give you answers.
The cave is full of the moon's red light and the star's purple glows.
In this cave lives the history of the world. The mind that lives in this
    cave belongs to everybody. It controls us.
Ask it questions and the answers will stick in your mind.
In the heavens above the moon lives God the creator from the
    beginning of time.

—*Andrew Vecchione*

The Secret of My Soul

Follow me up the path to nowhere.
Where the sky is black, the moon is red, and where my soul lives. It's
    the place where all questions are answered.
How did the sheep get their wool?
How does the moon fade out in the breeze?
How do people kill and why do they kill?
How do people feel when they are hurt?
My soul carries these secrets that only I know.

—*Andrew Vecchione*

49

I Hear Chevrolets Parking

Using "I Hear America Singing" as a Model

by Larry Fagin

Reading Walt Whitman again made me think that his poem "I Hear America Singing" would make a good starting point for a writing assignment for some third graders I'd been working with. Together we would create a catalog of all kinds of people singing their "varied carols." Maybe we'd have animals and inanimate things singing, too. I suggested that we start the poem off with Whitman's line "I hear America singing." Then we'd list who or what was singing—teacher, policeman, nurse, toaster oven—and what was being sung.

But. The kids wanted to make rhymes. They insisted that "I hear the bells ringing" be the next line. I gave in and the work became an exercise in Whitmanesque rhymed couplets. The first line of each couplet followed a format: "I hear (something) (making some sound)," e.g., "I hear the windows slamming." Then we'd get a rhyme (another participle) for the next line: "jamming," for example. Who or what was doing the jamming? "Jelly." In other words, in the second line of each couplet, we worked backwards, getting the rhyme first, and *then* the start of the line. This jumping around in the composition keeps the ideas and images fresh, as opposed to writing all the lines "straight out." Most of the couplets are about hearing (and sound), but some are about other senses. I suggested that all the poems begin and end with Whitman's title to give a sense of unity and closure.

I think these collaborations reflect Whitman's music and multifariousness even though I read the Whitman example only to the older (sixth-grade) students. The fact that they are collaborations by fifteen or more children makes them as diverse and populated as Whitman's poem.

I Hear America Singing

I hear America singing
I hear the bells ringing

I hear the glasses clinking
I hear the teachers drinking
I hear the drivers driving
I hear the nurses arriving
I hear water dripping
I hear my pants ripping
I hear the eggs frying
I hear the liars lying
I hear the mice squeaking
I hear the sneakers sneaking
I hear the ghosts booing
I hear the bunnies chewing
I hear the saw sawing
I hear the grandmas sewing
I hear the clock ticking
I hear feet kicking
I hear the pencils writing
I hear mosquitos biting
I hear the money jingling
I hear the spines tingling
I hear birds tweeting
I hear fat guys eating
I hear the chairs scraping
I hear prisoners escaping
I hear dreamers dreaming
I hear the babies screaming
I hear the tongues clicking
I hear the glue sticking
I hear Santa's stomach jiggling
I hear the girls giggling
I hear the lions roaring
I hear the grandpas snoring
I hear the poodles snapping
I hear the hands clapping
I hear the vines clinging
I hear America singing
            —*First-grade group*

I Hear America Singing

I hear America singing
I hear the bells ringing
I hear the cat scratching

51

I hear the fishermen catching
I hear the cars crashing
I hear potatoes mashing
I hear the cameras clicking
I hear the dogs licking
I hear the hearts beating
I hear cheaters cheating
I hear the firefly glowing
I hear the hair growing
I hear the owls screeching
I hear the teachers teaching
I hear the dryer drying
I hear blue jays flying
I hear the sun shining
I hear babies whining
I hear transformers transforming
I hear helicopters transporting
I hear buzzers buzzing
I feel the mothers hugging
I hear the pencil writing
I hear the boxers fighting
I hear Eskimos fishing
I hear the miller's daughter wishing
I hear bees stinging
I hear America singing
        —Third-grade group

I Hear America Singing

I hear America singing
I hear the bells ringing
I hear the tiger stalking
I hear the parrot talking
I hear the orange squeezing
I hear the Arctic freezing
I hear the dogs barking
I hear Chevrolets parking
I hear the babies crying
I hear the football flying
I hear the birds screeching
I feel the arms reaching
I hear the cat scratching
I hear the eggs hatching

I see the yuppies drinking
I hear the divers sinking
I hear the dolls dancing
I feel the eyes glancing
I hear the South Pacific splashing
I feel the potatoes mashing
I hear the blood flowing
I see the needles sewing
I hear the wind blowing
I hear the mowers mowing
I see the snow snowing
And the professors knowing
I hear the swings swinging
I hear America singing
        —Kindergarten and first-grade group

I Hear America Singing

I hear America singing
I hear the bells ringing
I hear rattlesnakes rattle
I hear the armies battle
I hear the people talking
I hear the children walking
I hear the birds flying
I hear babies crying
I hear rabbits jumping
I hear hearts pumping
I hear dancers stomping
I hear donuts dunking
I hear birds tweeting
I hear belts beating
I hear pages turning
I hear bushes burning
I hear throats coughing
I hear hyenas laughing
I hear pencils tapping
I hear flags flapping
I hear squirrels squeaking
I hear faucets leaking
I hear dogs barking
I hear cars parking
I hear beavers chopping
I hear mommies shopping

I hear rain falling
I hear grandmas calling
I hear pinballs rolling
I hear daddies bowling
I hear papers folding
I hear teachers scolding
I hear kangaroos bouncing
I hear eagles pouncing
I hear ants hustling
I hear cowboys rustling
I hear wolves howling
I hear bears growling
I hear the stars twinkling
I hear the cakes sprinkling
I hear cigarettes smoking
I hear the clowns joking
I hear windows slamming
I hear jelly jamming
I hear grown-ups arguing
I hear chefs bar-b-queing
I hear the trumpets swinging
I hear America singing
    —Third-grade group

I Hear America Singing

I hear America singing
I hear the doorbells ringing
I smell the turkeys cooking
I see big brown eyes looking
I hear the fingers picking
I feel the dobermans licking
I hear the grandmas knitting
I see the kiddies kidding
I hear the Swatches ticking
I watch Daryl Strawberry hitting
I see the green eyes blinking
And blue eyes winking
I feel my old brain thinking
I see the Titanic sinking
I feel my stomach aching
Because I ate too much of my mother's baking
The sunburned skin is peeling
My father is fixing a hole in the ceiling

I see the customers eating
I see the noses bleeding
The fishermen are fishing
I hear the cat's tail swishing
I feel the fingernails scratching
I see the chickens hatching
And soldiers are attacking
I see the actors acting
I hear Uncle Louie snoring
The bulls are goring
Mrs. Conroy is teaching
One student is cheating
I see the dreamers dreaming
I hear my neighbor screaming
I see the moonlight beaming
Christmas bulbs are gleaming
I hear the lungs breathing
And babies are teething
I feel the bees stinging
I hear America singing
                    —*Sixth-grade group*

Crafty Lures

Using Whitman's "There Was a Child Went Forth"

by Dale Worsley

Walt Whitman's "There Was a Child Went Forth" from *Leaves of Grass* is an excellent poem to use as an example to stimulate writing. I have used it in third- and sixth-grade classrooms in New York City schools, but it could be adapted for use with students of any age in any situation. Elementary school children respond well because it is about children, the plants and animals they see, the people they know, their homes, their feelings, and the landscapes around them.

After trying several approaches, I developed one that worked well. I explained that Whitman was a poet famous for writing about himself, and how great it was to be alive. Through his poetry he shows us that our *selves* aren't only what is inside our skin, but what comes in through our senses, too: "There was a child went forth every day. / And the first object he looked upon, that object he became." How can you *become* an object? The question is interesting philosophically. Many students, including third graders, seem to have a visceral understanding of the issue. A boy knocked on his desk. Now that desk was definitely inside him. In a way our eyes, ears, and other sense organs can "eat" things and take them in. When we take them in, we become them in our minds and memories.

We often discussed the importance of loving oneself. Today in many schools the issue is critical, and the students are sobered by the idea that the drug use and violence in their neighborhoods is linked to a lack of self-love. They themselves may feel unloved. Whitman is a poet from a century ago speaking directly to one of the central concerns of their lives today: how they feel about themselves.

I sometimes told the students that since Whitman had explained what the lives of children were like long ago, we might imagine he was waiting up in heaven to hear what their lives are like now. Before we started, though—before I even read the poem to them—I wanted them to see for themselves how his flowing style of writing worked, so I asked questions that focused them on the accretion of details necessary to create such currents of words:

"What do you see when you walk out of your house in the morning?"

"Cars."

"What kind of cars?"

"Nissan."

"Who's driving the Nissan?"

"A guy."

"What's he wearing?"

"A business suit."

"Where's he going?"

"To work."

"Where does he work?"

"In an office."

"To write like Whitman," I concluded, "you might say, 'When I leave my house in the morning I see men in business suits driving their Nissans to their offices.'"

Details, and lots of them. They make all the difference, especially when one is writing about the everyday. They are the difference between "my teacher" and "my teacher with long red fingernails and a picture of a kitten on her desk."

Whitman wrote his poem in the third person; I instructed the students to write in the first, to tell him about themselves. And not only about themselves just now, but themselves over a lifetime. How long would they remember that businessman in the Nissan? The schoolteacher? They would remember different things for different lengths of time. If they stopped and thought about it, no matter their young age, they had already incorporated some things in their memories longer than others. Their first bike? They might still remember it now, but forget it by the time they grew up. On the other hand, they would never forget their mother. The whole idea of a self being a fluid thing changing over time was put by Whitman in the next lines: "And that object became a part of him for the day or a certain part of the day, / Or for many years or stretching cycles of years."

I divided the poem into four parts (disregarding Whitman's own divisions), to be introduced one after the other in four writing sessions. The first part was about plants and animals, from "The early lilacs became part of this child" to "And the apple trees cover'd with blossoms and the fruit afterward, and wood-berries, and the commonest weeds by the road."

The students were eager to have some of the odd words and ideas explained: "pink-faint litter" (they could just envision those piglets), "suspending" (wasn't it amazing how fish could hang in the water). I asked how many had been to farms, and always, even though some of the classes were in the inner city, most of the students had. (I would never have predicted so many had petted a foal, identified birds, picked apples. It pays never to make assumptions. One seemingly macho boy knew about flowers: four o'clocks and cosmos were his favorites.) The younger children in particular were warmed by the mention of young animals. After we talked about Whitman's animals and ones the students had seen on farms, we talked about the plants and animals they saw in the city: the crows, blue jays and pigeons (and the parrots—many had parrots), the grass, the trees, the flowers. Even in as unnatural an environment as New York City, when one focuses on the weeds in empty lots and in cracks in the cement, and the trees planted along the curbs, and the window boxes and flowerpots on fire escapes, one may see a great deal of natural life.

After discussion, the students wrote for ten straight minutes any thoughts that came into their minds about the plants and animals in their lives. I felt it was important to keep them writing continuously, so if they stopped, I goaded, cajoled, and encouraged them to keep going. Many were inhibited by problems with spelling, or the fear of expressing their ideas, so I discouraged erasing, while allowing crossing-out if they moved right on. (At the end of class I gave them the opportunity to tell me words that needed to be corrected and I wrote them on the blackboard. We called this our daily "spellfest.") They responded well, quickly becoming accustomed to the process of writing with the flow of the mind.

•

The second section of "There Was a Child Went Forth," like the first and the subsequent two, was something to which I devoted an entire class period: first reading and talking about the words and ideas in the section, then relating the ideas to the children's world, then having the children write. We read from "And the old drunkard, staggering home from the outhouse from which he had lately risen" to "And all the changes of city and country wherever he went."

It was necessary to explain that times were different then. Women teachers were called "schoolmistresses." The students found it amusing to discuss their own teachers in the context of a poem. As for the "barefoot negro boy and girl," I explained that many kids back then had no shoes, but the ground was safer, with fewer broken bottles and no hot asphalt. I skipped the word "negro" for convenience's sake, not wanting to be sidetracked at this point by a long discussion of racial issues. (I did discuss these issues later.) Once the kids thought about it, they realized they knew a wide variety of different people, from postal workers to doctors, the poor to the wealthy.

In one school a girl wrote a piece about drug addicts killing each other, about nightly shootings, about a fat man being dragged into the shadows to be killed, about women stabbing and killing each other. When she finished she said, "This is not writing," tore it up and threw it away. I salvaged it, and subsequently grabbed her papers before she could destroy them, until she felt confident enough to write about anything, including both the horrible things that were in the front of her mind, and the more pleasant things that followed. I was distressed that so many other third graders also described so much violence. Once the disturbing images were released, however, more hopeful ones almost always followed.

•

The third section, about parents, ran from "His own parents, he that father'd him and she that had conceiv'd him in her womb and birth'd him" to "Whether that which appears so is so, or is it all flashes and specks?"

This section was somewhat tricky, and raised interesting issues. Whitman describes what would today perhaps be known as an abusive father. If, in response to this section, a student had described abuse at home, I would have had a dilemma altogether too common in the modern classroom: when, how, and to whom to report the crime. But none of my students did. They were more interested in the way Whitman pointed out how adults strike "tight bargains" with them and use "crafty lures" ("You can have dessert if you finish your lima beans"). Another issue that seemed to intrigue the students, though very little of their writing actually addressed it directly, was the idea of doubt ("Is it all flashes and specks?"). The students seemed comforted by the idea that all people doubt, that it's a normal part of life. Finally I stressed the importance of the familiar, quotidian things—how beautiful one's kitchen table can be, one's sofa, one's bed. The kids were excited by the idea of describing their homes and relatives, and in general did so in innocent, loving, and discreet ways.

•

I described the last section (the remainder of the poem) as having to do with landscapes. Indeed the section is like a painting, with its descriptions of color and light, so I often drew a rough outline on the board. I always had to define the term "horizon." Most students had never been asked to look at their environments as landscapes: i.e., the big things, the far things, the many details together. They were interested in the difference between landscapes then and landscapes now. It seemed as though the children became more farseeing when we talked about distant villages, seashores, ferries, schooners, roofs and gables, and they wrote eagerly about the landscape features they knew, such as skyscrapers, public beaches, subways, airplanes, and housing projects.

•

Many benefits came of the four Whitman exercises derived from this one poem. If the students never developed their initial writing into poems or stories, they still carried away the feeling that *their* worlds, inside and out, were important, that as children they were valued, and that self and world were both worth a great deal of thought and writing. They learned how fluid their writing could become, how natural, easy, all-encompassing. The attention spans of many students grew dramatically when they entered the stream-of-consciousness mode. The rhythms of the sentences in the poems were compelling. The students became encouraged by their own increasing ability to describe, using the evocative power of detail. By expressing their feelings honestly and openly like Whitman, they felt better. By sharing their writing, they discovered new things about each other and respected each other more.

In some of the classes I held chain-readings, in which one student would read a few sentences, and I would move on to another student, then another, as they sat at their desks. This type of reading worked for a while, but then deteriorated into all the students wanting to read and none wanting to listen. I realized that this was a concept more for my own gratification than for theirs (I wanted a rousing Ode-to-Joy choral effect). More straightforward readings, where students were able to stand in front of the class and deliver an entire, edited poem, worked better. Despite our limited time, which usually allowed each student to read only once, many wanted to read twice.

One teacher, of a class that had been labeled slow (just above the English as a Second Language group), said to me, "You're getting them to write. This is a milestone. They're not s-t-u-p-i-d. They're afraid of writing, and this helps them overcome their fear." Whitman's poetry usually helps everyone overcome their fear.

Some students included their "Whitman" poems in the student anthologies. Here are a few examples:

(The first four pieces are by sixth-grade students in P.S. 190 in Manhattan.)

From Whitman

When I go to school
I see
women & men running
to catch a bus.
I see
teachers
with their sunglasses
and long black raincoats,
their red nail polish
and gold jewelry.
I see
crossing guards with a

white banner helping
children.
I see
my building super
putting garbage bags in
garbage cans
with his gray gloves
and blue jacket.
I see
other children going to school.
They have their lunch boxes
and bookbags.
I see
people with
briefcases and suits
talking to their
friends
with their red
skirts and high-heel shoes.
I see
people from all over the world
talking in different languages
with white scarves
around their heads.
When I go to school
I see
things that become a part of me.
   —Consuelo Posloncec

From Whitman

The cab driver with the long, black, uncut hair,
 with the backwards baseball cap,
 with the expired license that was supposed to be renewed
  two years ago.
The custodian who always points at the ceiling.
 He has a big shiny head and a wet mop.
The principal with two fingers always up,
 with a nice dress and shirt. . . .
   —Jeffrey Olsen

From Whitman

When I leave my house in the summer, I see the beautiful flowers with the best smell and the best colors on them, colors that you can't imagine. When I see them it makes me happy and brings out the joy that is somewhere inside of me. Flowers are more than just something that sits there. They mean everything to me. If I have nobody to talk to, I can go to a flower. It won't tell you you are wrong and it won't tell you you're right. It just listens to me. Sometimes I even think it is really listening to me. The flower I like talking to best is a rose, a red, good-smelling, good-looking rose. The sight of them can just amaze you, the way their petals open and close, the way they grow and live and even the way they die.
　　　—*Tara*

When I Go to School

When I go to school
　　my danger alarm is on.
I see all sorts of mystic things
like drugs on every corner,
gangs fighting one another
　　like in the past,
posses crying for help
　　as the cops pull them away,
crossing guards acting like
　　a parent,
firemen trying to stop
　　fires from hell,
cops getting hurt and shot for
　　trying to break up a fight,
drug dealers trying to take
　　a life for money,
kids locking out their own fears,
business people going to
　　try to succeed in life,
teachers who try to make this
　　world a better place,
parents in constant fear
　　for their children's lives,
bums living a shameful life. . . .
　　　—*Dameon J. Claytor*

(The following pieces are by third-grade students at P.S. 152 in Brooklyn.)

The People I See

These are the people I see
around me: I see the police
around me. I see bums.
I see guards. I see
babies walking
to school. I see
cats. I see dogs.
I see houses.
I see people
walking their children
to school.
I see horses.
I see sneakers.
I see men going
to work.
I see cars.
My little brother
is a pest.
My sister
is a pest.
I love lamb chops.
I like bar-b-que.
I love my grandmother.
        —*Hanzel Walker*

I See

I see one black crow
chirping as the wind goes by.
I see famous women,
multiplication chart 14681012.
I see a chalkboard, spelling test.
I see a globe, an American flag,
my teacher, book reports,
a television.
I see Deborah, Frank, Ludshy, Chris,
Melissa, Tanya—I see Ephraim
yawning and stretching.

I see Cornell sleeping
on his notebook.
I see spelling words
and ABCs all over the wall.
The people who are a part of me are:
Vaughn making faces, Deborah thinking,
Candace talking to Ludshy,
Sandra A. counting,
Frank looking at Charles,
Damaris talking to Tanya,
Cornell with a hurting eye,
Chris, Melissa, Dave, June, Vaughn,
Mario, Robert,
Sandra working.
Everybody's working
with beautiful handwriting,
June with a jumpsuit on.
Nancy Reagan, Sandra Day O'Connor,
Lady Bird Johnson, Eleanor Roosevelt,
Barbara Walters, Beverly Sills,
Joan Ganz Cooney. . . all of those
are famous women and there's more!
       —*Ebony Reid*

I'm Leaving

When I'm leaving the house
I see trees, a car in my driveway,
the Languars, my next-door neighbors,
getting in their car.
I get in the car with my mother
and father, and when we're riding,
we pass the toy store, the sneaker store,
the grocery store, the candy store,
the Capital store, then Brooklyn College,
then a couple of houses, and then I see
yellow, white, green, blue, red,
fuschia, orange, purple, pink flowers.
I see crows, hawks, parrots, ducks,
baby chicks, bees buzzing.
I see Mr. Dale leaving. I'm
passing Brooklyn College.
I see school. Bye. I'm going.
       —*Candace Mealy*

At the Beach

When I go to the beach
I see white and brown ducks
that sail in the water
like beautiful floating boats.
And I see the water splash
as the shells come and go.
The sand is like a balloon
floating in the sky.
The beach is as beautiful
as the rainbow umbrella
that blocks the sun.
I love the beach.
It is a lovely place to be.
       —Keisha Constance

People

Plants are sometimes covered with ants
and bees buzz a wonderful song as long
as the day lasts, with the squirrels
scattering in the pretty green grass,
and birds feeding their young.
The trees sway in the wind
as it blows firmly.
As the children play I play with my dog
all the way home, and all day.
The people I see and the people
who are with me. . . there are people
surrounding me. . . dangerous people,
homeless people,
and many many more people,
people from other countries,
for example: India, Asia, Spain,
and European people.
And the junkman chasing girls
in the dark and dirty alleys.
The weird-looking people
who walk in the building.
The people around who live different lives.
People sometimes act stupid.

There are people who cry
and people who fly airplanes.
There are good people and bad people.
    —*Jamal Wood*

Don't Tell Me That I Talk Too Much

I see lots of things
when school is over.
I go out and see
lots of things,
like the shine of the sun.
I feel good.
I see the beautiful singing bird
flying in the warm air.
I see cats looking for good food.
I see children playing lots of games.
I see lots of trees, like oak trees.
I feel the warm air.
I go to the beach.
I see the water waving around,
nice and soft.
I go swimming.
Whee! It feels good.
I feel the sand, good and very soft.
I feel the wet soft snow in my hand.

Teaching "The Sleepers" to Younger Children

by *William Bryant Logan*

My third and fourth graders are addicted to the verbs "go," "do," "say," and "be." I use Walt Whitman's "The Sleepers" to get them inspired about other action words. The poem is full of sleep: everyone and everything sleeping, and the poet able to sense and see the sleeping of them all. My students and I write poems that, like "The Sleepers," repeat one strong verb in many different ways.

When I work with "The Sleepers," I use most of the first thirty-one lines down through "And I become the other dreamers." The constant repetition of the word "sleep" (in lines 12–23) is delightful to us as we read the section, and we talk about how a rhythm is created by that dependable word returning in line after line. We notice how full and exact the lines are, including everyone from the peaceful husband and wife to the condemned murderer. I also discuss the poet's mind, not only his sympathy for everyone, but also the openness of a mind that, when it doesn't know something, asks a question about it: "And the murdered person . . . . How does he sleep?"

Next, we make a list on the blackboard of all the actions that we might want to be able to see the way Whitman sees sleep. It's fun, almost a poem in itself: jump, laugh, yell, roll, fly, command, flip, dance, giggle, fish, run, walk, swim, whisper. All by itself, this list gives us an entrance into Whitman's paradoxically full but always spacious world, a world of action and possibility.

Because this poem uses line-by-line repetition, it's a natural to try out first as an oral collaboration. Sometimes, I write the children's lines on the board, sometimes just let them flow by. When all the children's minds are working together, the results are strange and beautiful. Here, for example, is "The Swimmers" (The Spanish in the last line means "come here"):

The red bugs are swimming.
Mrs. Glenn is swimming in the Bronx.
Animals are swimming in the sea.

Mr. Logan was swimming at the beach with a crab monster.
Bruce Lee is swimming, swimming in the Pacific Ocean.
Swim, swam, swum . . . Where is the bum?
My brother, he swims, swims, swims. . . .
President Gorbachev is swimming in the classroom.
A sound. Is it swimming in my ear?
My mother swims in the hot blue water.
The seahorse . . . it dies, it comes alive and it swims in the sea.
My guitar is swimming in the sea.
"Ven aca!" it sings.

Whitman wrote that he wanted his poems to express the fullness of his own personality. It's interesting to see that, imitating him, third and fourth graders can give such a full portrait of their own wishes, wonder, cantankerousness, affections, and fears.

If the collaborations show the personality of a class, the individual poems let the students take what tone and attitude they will. I ask each of them to choose one action word—whether from the board or not—and to use the word as much as they can to make a poem that is full of the action. The variety of results is surprising. One student, obsessed by questions, writes a whole scary poem of questions about hanging, beginning, "Does the girl hang peacefully by her ponytail?" Melody Prosser stuffs her poem full of forms of the word giggle. Another student writes about a foot race between Carl Lewis, a goldfish, a dolphin, and a lamppost. Occasionally, a writer elects to use all the words on the board, like Makeda Benjamin in her piece about crazy action. Tanya James writes an extraordinary poem about her jumping heart and jumping frogs.

More than most imitations, these pieces seem to belong to the kids, since Whitman's breathless way of writing is similar to the way children think when they're excited. I find that the kids not only enjoy writing these poems, but that they enjoy performing them for the class. The oral energy is already in the poems, waiting to burst out.

My mommy is a giggler.
My father is a giggler.
Sam's a giggler.
Buck's a giggler.
The man of my dreams is a giggler and a giggler.
The frog is giggling.

I don't know if the pig is giggling.
Ronald Reagan. Is he giggling?
Even I giggle and giggle and giggle.
    —*Melody Prosser*

My fingers are playing football with each other,
and my nose is dancing, and my toes are playing handgames,
and my heart is swimming in my veins.
My lips are smacking.
My teeth are having lunch and turning yellow.
Shoes are running down the street.
And the fruits are jumping into people's mouths.
It was raining clocks and plops on my block.
And the crayons are scribbling graffiti on the subway. . . .
    —*Makeda Benjamin*

My heart jumps every time I breathe
and jumps faster every time I run.
And every time little girls jump and sing
My heart goes the same beat.
Frogs jump into a blue pond,
and my heart jumps into a red pond
that's inside me. It seems
like my heart tells them to come to me.
They're jumping into each other's ponds,
because they're related to each other.
My heart jumps into the frog's blue pond,
and the frogs jump into my red pond.
    —*Tanya James*

The "I" Is Another

by Anne Waldman

Walt Whitman's poem "The Sleepers" opens with the line "I
wander all night in my vision" and proceeds to describe the poet's
travels in his nocturnal imagination. With unflagging enthusiasm, he pictures a host of colorful sleepers, meeting them "face
to face," "bending with open eyes" over their "shut eyes": children
in cradles, drunkards, married couples, corpses, "sacred idiots,"
and the blind. Moving from bedside to bedside, he lists a great
variety of slumberers. Then, as if exemplifying Arthur Rimbaud's
"I is another," he expands further, empathizing with all of them:
actor, actress, voter, politician, emigrant, exile, stammerer,
male and female, beloved and lover, requited and unrequited.
There is a wonderful and unexpected moment when his excitement drives him further into his poem:

O hotcheeked and blushing! O foolish hectic!
O for pity's sake, no one must see me now! . . . . my clothes were
    stolen while I was abed,
Now I am thrust forward, where shall I run?

Many of us have had similar dreams of finding ourselves seri-
ously underdressed.

    The next section of the poem is different. In it, none of the
figures are sleeping, and the poet descends not into sleep but into
death. Whitman suddenly ages and identifies with an old woman
darning her grandson's socks, next with a "sleepless widow
looking out on the winter midnight," then with the light of the
stars glittering on the snow. The cold and pallor of the snow lead
him to seeing a shroud, and, with typical Whitmanic magic, he
becomes the shroud, on a corpse underground. Like the tribal
shaman (or anyone who has just gotten a good report after a
scary visit to the doctor), the one who returns from the under-
world tells the living to value what they have: "It seems to me
that everything in the light and air ought to be happy; / Whoever
is not in his coffin and the dark grave, let him know he has
enough."

The third section describes a "beautiful gigantic swimmer" who struggles against sea waves that bash him around until he drowns. This peculiar and haunting section sounds as though it might have come from one of Whitman's own dreams.

Section 4 is something of a continuation of section 3: "I turn but do not extricate myself." Standing on a beach, the poet witnesses a shipwreck at night: "I hear the burst as she strikes . . I hear the howls of dismay. . . ." He searches the beach "with the crowd," and in the morning helps "pick up the dead and lay them in rows in a barn."

The fifth section begins with more death imagery (a description of George Washington weeping over the slaughter of his young soldiers) but it veers off into what sounds like a tableau vivant of the General bidding good-bye to his army. Whitman doesn't tell us whether these are dream scenes or historical scenes that, in the memory, take on the aura of dreams.

He is more explicit in section 6: "Now I tell what my mother told me today as we sat at dinner together." One morning, when his mother was still living at home with her parents, an astonishingly beautiful Indian woman wandered in and stayed until the middle of the afternoon, and then she left, never to be seen again. His mother had wanted her to stay, and missed her terribly, and remembered her all those years. The section concludes with a curse against Lucifer, who separates people, who interferes and permeates all experience with death.

As if the poet has had enough of death, section 7 builds into a quiet ode to the beauty of all the dreaming persons the poet has observed in his peripatetic vision. The poem is infused with "love and summer," and everything is made right: the immigrants and exiles return to their homelands, where they are welcomed warmly. Everyone is made equal and restored, made beautiful in the "dim night," individuals united in a cosmic peace.

But Whitman goes even further; in section 8 he joins whole continents together:

The Asiatic and African are hand in hand . . the European and
    American are hand in hand,
Learned and unlearned are hand in hand . . and male and female are
    hand in hand.

These repetitions have a lulling, soothing effect, as this section

72

rises into an ecstatic hymn of "matings." The sexes embrace, parents embrace children, teachers students, masters slaves. The ill are restored to health: the insane become sane, the paralyzed supple. Whitman's vision performs miracles! His voice is vatic—exorcizing evil, embracing the cosmos, healing those in strife and pain—but, at the same time, surprisingly down-to-earth.

The closing lines of "The Sleepers" invoke and salute the night that is the archetypal Mother, the poet's muse, the *sine qua non* for what has happened in the poem. The poet himself was "yielded" (born) from night. Night has allowed his illumination of a unified and perfected humanity, and so he acknowledges his muse's power.

"The Sleepers" is a fairly straightforward poem. Its language is accessible. In his open letter to Emerson, included in the second edition of *Leaves of Grass*, Whitman proclaimed that he would "meet people and The States face to face"—the way he meets the sleepers in the poem—"to confront them with an American rude tongue," by which he meant ordinary, vernacular language. The poem is also straightforward in that it comes directly from the poet's heart. Without the intermediary of symbols or "literary" maneuvering, the reader experiences both the trajectory of a powerful revelation and his or her own place in it. Whitman's vision is of a true democracy, in which our strength is a "unity in diversity." There is room for everyone in this attractive, healing vision, in which everyone in the entire world is in love with everyone else.

We can't be sure how the poem was composed, but because "The Sleepers" is a rather long poem, it would have been difficult to write in one sitting. Notice the shifts in mood between the different sections, and how the poem picks up the same theme again and again, but introduces and colors it in different ways. Although it has an undeniable flow and continuity, it starts and stops. It reiterates constantly. Notice, too, how within stanzas Whitman uses dots, dashes, semicolons, and colons to keep the poem moving along, and how he uses periods (or other stop punctuation) at the end of each stanza. For example, the first stanza of section 8 (which includes fourteen very long lines) opens with "The sleepers are very beautiful as they lie unclothed" and proceeds to describe those sleepers in a list that is enhanced by punctuation that keeps the flow alive and fluid, as in:

The felon steps forth from the prison . . . . the insane becomes sane
. . . . the suffering of sick persons is relieved,
The sweatings and fevers stop . . . the throat that was unsound is
sound . . . the lungs of the consumptive are resumed . . . the poor
distressed head is free . . .

eventually moving to a last line that calls the whole stanza together in a final end-stop: "They pass the invigoration of the night and the chemistry of the night and awake." After a breath, the next stanza's opening line shifts the focus abruptly to the personal "I": "I too pass from the night." Whitman also varies the pace of his poem by questioning and exclaiming, as in "The murderer that is to be hung next day . . . . how does he sleep? / And the murdered person . . . . how does he sleep?" or "What are you doing you ruffianly red-trickled waves?" and "I am a dance . . . . Play up there! the fit is whirling me fast" or "O love and summer! you are in the dreams and in me." He also skillfully exercises the present tense throughout, giving the poem its immediacy, timelessness, and "averaging" aspect. We are thrust into a permanent state of inspiring—and ironically active—slumber.

Read "The Sleepers" the way it was written: with feelings and senses open. Feel the pulse of the language, the heave of Whitman's lines. (You could read it aloud solo or with others reading individual lines.) As you read, visualize the sleepers, as Whitman does; let your mind and imagination expand. Try not to hold back. You might make a list of the active verbs he uses—almost all his verbs, as noted, are in the present tense. Notice how he uses the pronoun "I" and how that contrasts with his descriptions of others. Notice also how we move back and forth from his imagined and projected vision to his more experiential "personal" vision. The former is all-inclusive; the latter seems linked particularly to the poet's own psychological need to reshape the world through the act of writing. Do we share the same need, or is it enough to be included in his fantasy of a united humanity? It is intriguing to think about where we are situated, as audience. Between the two? Somewhere between sleeping and waking?

An interesting writing experiment is to write a piece focusing on a theme (as Whitman did with sleep), some common human activity. Take running, for example, and make a big list

of runners that you have seen and that you can imagine. Or imagine all the people you can think of working at desks. Start each line with a simple "I see" or "I watch." Write down the "minute particulars" of what you visualize. Let your mind free-associate (or, as Whitman called it, "wander"). In your first draft, don't be afraid of being too grandiose, panoramic, all-encompassing, even sentimental; you can always change it later. Jump into the maelstrom of humanity, as Whitman does.

Poet of the Crowd
by Mark Statman

Whitman writes so brilliantly, so completely, about what he hears and smells, what he sees, tastes and touches. He walks through New York (or any city) and he reports it to you as it happens:

Ever the hard unsunk ground
Ever the eaters and drinkers, ever the upward and downward sun, ever
    the air and the ceaseless tides,
Ever myself and my neighbors, refreshing, wicked, real . . .
This is the city and I am one of the citizens . . .
                    (from "Song of Myself")

His involvement with the world around him—his journalistic instincts to look and question ("Not words of routine this song of mine, / But abruptly to question, to leap beyond but nearer bring")—is something I've always wanted to bring to my own work: poetry not necessarily as transformative (what world do I imagine?) but poetry as reportorial (just what, out there, is it important that I see?). And how my students are involved with the world is something I've always asked them to think about and become interested in. I haven't taught Whitman in the schools lately, but that's because I've been working with a lot of African-American and Latino children (K–2), and I've been interested in using the work of poets from those cultures. But some of the things which have inspired me in Whitman (descriptions, lists, driving rhythms and repetitions, openness to people and to the city and country, the desire to feel the spiritual in the physical) are also in the works of poets I've used in class (such as Octavio Paz, Margaret Walker, Mayra Jiménez, Sergio Mondragon, Pablo Neruda, and Federico García Lorca, some of whom were directly influenced by Whitman) and in the responses from my students:

To the Stars

Hello stars
Please don't look to me
Look to the flowers
Color blue color brown color red
Color to orange color yellow
Color to the moon is blue
Color to corazón red
Today is Friday Hello Karla
Hello Mark
to the Christmas Mark
to Connecticut
               —*Karla Pascual Cordova, second grade*

I feel great in the summer
The sun shines on
all the flowers and
on all the earth and on
the brown houses
It shines in my window
across my chair and the
floor and on me
It makes me warm and
I think of the sand
and crawling crabs at
the beach
               —*Richard P., first grade*

Freddy Krueger sees the spring
He sees the clouds and girls
He hears rap songs
oh yeah oh yeah oh
He likes to kiss girls
but the girls are scared
of him.
               —*Claude Reed, first grade*

Whitman influenced my poetry and my teaching, but I think
it's more as a reader of him that I've wanted him around so much

of the time. I do a lot of traveling in Mexico and in Central and South America, and whenever I go I always carry a complete poems of Keats or a complete Whitman (the beautiful, durable Penguin edition with the Thomas Eakins painting on the cover). Both poets have their appeal, the dynamic visions, the complex relationships they draw between the way one experiences the world and the way one desires to experience it. Both poets reduce the tensions of travel: the problems of being alone, the danger, uncertainty, and fear. I think I bring the Keats as a way of projecting myself into another place, as a way of thinking not about where I am at the moment, but where I could be, how I could be.

With Whitman, I get something else entirely. Because Whitman has a mysterious way of reconnecting me with others, of making me feel that no matter where I am, I'll always find people to be with and places to go, I'll always be all right. That is his assurance for those who take any kind of risk:

O my brave soul!
O farther farther sail!
O daring joy, but safe! are they not all the seas of God?
O farther farther farther sail!
　　　(*from* "Passage to India")

Before I began to write this, I had a flash, sort of a series of crazy newsreels of myself in various South American cities: worried and uncertain during an earthquake in Lima, Peru; exhausted and depressed in overcast Esmeraldas, Ecuador; stuck in a bleak SRO in San José, Costa Rica; alone and lonely in Cartagena, Colombia. What I remember is that during all these times, I picked up my Whitman, I read and read and read, and suddenly the world around me became very familiar. I saw the warmth in the faces of the people of Lima as we all struggled to make sense of what had just happened. I drank beer with fishermen on the Ecuadoran coast and talked about politics and the sea. In San José I went to markets, bought bread and fruit. I talked to hammock sellers and beer vendors, to women selling monkeys and jewelry on a brilliant Colombian beach. Each of these times, through the voice of Whitman, I could hear the voices of others. I could listen and talk, could see, taste and feel. Wherever I was, I felt at home.

Whitman's Own Way

The Poet as Role Model

by William Bryant Logan

Remember that spate of bumper stickers about Real Men? "Real Men Don't Eat Quiche," etc. Most of us could summarize our lives as a collection of such bumper stickers, the received ideas that we accept as if they were God's Own Truth. The years from the middle of primary school through high school are a crucible of peer pressure and psychological self-examination, where "bumper sticker life" is powerfully distilled. There is something unique in every child, but under the relentless pressure to fit in, it often gets buried or goes cold.

Wouldn't it be a good thing, if in those rough years, a young person had a hero who was courageous enough to go his own way? I am thinking particularly of those adolescents who may feel their differentness and be ashamed of it. As I recall, my heroes of that time were first Madame Curie and later Cyrano de Bergerac, but I wish I'd known about Walt Whitman.

Here was a man whom the polite society of his day abhorred, but who persisted in seeking the highest and the sweetest in himself. He was called things like "that bad man," "a sexual predator," a man suffering from "want of education and delicate feelings," "a charlatan," "a solemn humbug," and a "decidedly disreputable person." James Russell Lowell declared, "I will take care to keep (his book) out of the way of students." But the wonderful thing about Whitman is that despite the pressure to form his personality in reaction to what others thought of him, he made a positive virtue of living as he wished.

The temptations to do otherwise could hardly have been stronger. The son of a morose sometime carpenter, Whitman had many reasons to identify with a peer group as quickly as possible. Of the seven children born to Louisa and Walter Whitman, Sr., two went mad and one was retarded. The family never lived in one place more than a year, the father building or renovating homes, then seeking to sell them before the banks foreclosed. In the mid-nineteenth-century financial panics, he often lost out. Furthermore, the New York of Whitman's later adolescence was not always a comfortable place. As Justin Kaplan described it in his fine biography of the poet, "Pigs scavenged in the Broadway gutters and were set upon by packs of homeless dogs; troops of ragged child prostitutes, twelve and younger, haunted the crossings; thieves and pickpockets darted through the crowds." The picture is eerily like that of urban life today. What is a sane young person to do? Find acceptance through a social life of sex, alcohol, or drugs? Join a cult? Love money and influence? Develop a lasting cynicism towards life?

Whitman did none of these things. In fact, by the standards of his society, he became a resounding failure. An apostle of the virtues of sexual love, he was himself nearly celibate. He never had a career, to speak of, but worked now as a teacher, now a printer, now a journalist, now an editor, now a shopkeeper, now a political orator, now a real estate speculator, now a government clerk. He could play fast and loose with money he was loaned or given: one creditor took him to court over a $200 loan; money raised to help him buy a house when he was an aged invalid, he spent instead on the construction of his elaborate tomb. The enthusiasms of his intellectual life, popular as they were at the time, were not the sort of thing a literary man built his reputation on: he went in for phrenology (the study of a man's character according to the size and shape of his head), Egyptology, and semioccult sciences.

His own great book, *Leaves of Grass*, never found an established publisher during his lifetime: first it was distributed by a phrenological business, then by a fledgling Boston firm, and when that company went under, by the poet himself. Not that he was modest about the book: he wrote glowing, anonymous reviews of it in New York newspapers, and when Ralph Waldo Emerson wrote him a letter praising the book, Whitman promptly printed and distributed the letter without Emerson's permission.

So what makes Whitman anything more than, at best, a charming eccentric? First, of course, he was right in his own sanguine assessment of *Leaves of Grass*. Though some of the nineteenth-century literary lions of America held him at arm's length—Longfellow, Lowell, and Whittier disliked his poems—his work, not theirs, has survived as living poetry today. In its rough music, its exactness, its wide reach, his poetry created a new standard that no American poet can ignore and that no American poet has surpassed.

But the poems are such because the life was such. In the preface to the first edition of *Leaves of Grass*, Whitman set out a program for the American poet, concerned less with rhythm and reading than with a manner of life. "This is what you shall do," he wrote. "Love the earth and the sun and the animals, despise riches, give alms to every one that asks, stand up for the stupid and crazy, devote your income and labor to others, hate tyrants, argue not concerning God, have patience and indulgence toward the people, take off your hat to nothing known or unknown or to any man or number of men, go freely with powerful uneducated persons and the young and with the mothers of families, [. . .] re-examine all you have been told at school or in church or in any book, dismiss whatever insults your own soul, and your very flesh shall be a great poem not only in its words but in the silent lines of its lips and face and between the lashes of your eyes and in every motion and joint of your body. . . . "

It isn't hard to hold such romantic ideals; what is difficult is to try to live them. Yet there is good evidence that Whitman did. He could talk to anyone, from a ferryman to a philosopher, on equal terms. The "indolence" that some employers complained of, came from Whitman's habit of spending a lot of time on the streets, riding up front with the trolley drivers, walking Broadway, talking to all and sundry. He had no stifling conception of himself as a Personage, except insofar as he longed to be "vast," to contain "multitudes." He liked himself ("There is that lot of me, and all so luscious!"), and consequently, he could like others.

Whitman particularly liked men and boys (see the unforgettable portraits of the twenty-eight swimmers in section 11 of "Song of Myself"). Yet he resisted attempts, even by his ardent admirers, to equate his affection with homosexual love. Who knows what he and his men friends did in the privacy of their rooms, but what he called for was "adhesiveness"—a phrenological term, meaning open and unashamed friendship, symbolized by two women embracing—and he claimed the right for men to behave as affectionately towards one another as did women.

As for his work habits, though he was dismissed several times for "indolence," the newspapers of New York continued to hire him—more than once as top editor—because he could sling political fire and brimstone with the best of them, and perhaps too because he was a trained printer who understood how a paper was put together, from the type to the sheet. He was not ashamed to curry favor when he needed work, but he lost one job for "kicking a politician down the stairs."

When he had money, he used it to support his family. In 1845, while he had the best job he'd ever have, as editor of the *Brooklyn Daily Eagle*, he cosigned the mortgage on the family's new house in Brooklyn and supplied regular living expenses. A decade later, he acted as manager of a building concern that employed his father and two of his brothers. On his death, he left the entire contents of his estate—including the plates of his books—to his retarded brother Eddy.

Almost a decade after the first publication of *Leaves of Grass*— with some literary reputation and a good deal of notoriety to his credit—Whitman chose to go to Washington and eventually become a government clerk. It was 1863, the middle of the Civil War. Washington was one big barracks and hospital. After much wrangling, he got the sinecure. Instead of retiring to his desk to write poems, however, he spent his days and nights in the military hospitals, visiting more than 100,000 wounded soldiers: talking with them, comforting them, writing their letters home. To finance the gifts of food, drink, and books that he brought them, he raised funds in Boston and New York, writing letters to any and all who might help him.

But Whitman never deliberately sought to become a saint. He had enough admirers late in his life who thought him some kind of guru. Yet maybe he is, to a greater degree than many, a model of what a Real Man should be: unafraid, generous, tender, working on what he cared for most. In his poems, too, he rejected the "curtains" of literary style, wanting not to impress but to invite: "What I tell I tell for precisely what it is. Let who may exalt or startle or fascinate or soothe I will have purposes as health or heat or snow has and be as regardless of observation. . . . You shall stand by my side and look in the mirror with me."

Such sentiments were unconvincing to the young Henry James, who called Whitman's "Drum-Taps" a "flashy imitation of ideas." Later, however, the great novelist reversed his opinion, declaring himself ashamed of the "little atrocity" he'd committed in that early review. Whitman, he concluded, was the greatest American poet. But more telling than this literary praise was the fact that James, imitating Whitman, brought gifts and solace to the wounded in military hospitals during the First World War.

In Whitman's poems and prose, James admired "the love of life plucked like a flower in a desert of innocent unconscious ugliness."

Teaching Whitman in High School
by Bill Zavatsky

My first sustained reading of Whitman took place in the fall of 1965 or the spring of 1966. It was his "Song of Myself," a good chunk of which I read while sitting in a lobby at the New School for Social Research in New York, waiting for a jazz improvisation class to begin. After three years at a small college in Connecticut, I had "dropped out" and worked for a year. When I resumed my education, I felt myself at a new beginning. Whitman confirmed my adventure—the new life on which I had embarked as well as the stirrings of a real commitment to writing, especially to poetry. That afternoon, at the New School, Whitman's rolling line forever fused itself to the long-lined solos of the jazz artists that I most admired; and all I had to do was look around me to see that he was one of the great poets of New York.

But more than this, Whitman's work touched experiences in me that had long been buried, experiences the nature of which I can only call spiritual. A few years ago, when I started teaching his poems to my tenth- and twelfth-grade English classes, it was because he was one of those writers who confirmed a sensation that, up through my teens, I had now and again felt: the gift of seeing everything in my range of vision with a startling clarity, as if whatever I turned my gaze toward was bathed in the beam of a powerful searchlight, but not at the expense of surrounding objects, which retained their focus. Concomitant with this heightened sense of vision was the sensation of being connected to all that I saw, joined to it in a oneness that both dazzled me and left me with a feeling of inner joy. These states did not last very long, and they were so extraordinary that I was afraid to investigate them, even to mention them. (They seemed qualitatively *different* from the feelings of piety or devotion or exaltation that I experienced as a Roman Catholic boy.) The manifestation was not linked to creed or dogma, but showered down upon me when I least expected it—on a spectacularly clear fall day, or a summer afternoon as I walked down a tree-lined street, heading home from a baseball game. All I knew was that it "happened," that I was grateful for this visitation, and that I would remember the effect that it had upon me.

Before my students and I read Whitman's poems, I introduce them to Whitman by describing these experiences. I have discovered that there is a hunger in young people—"religious" or not—to discuss "heightened" transpersonal experiences. In doing so I never feel that I am forcing a belief system on my students. For example, as I gave my little personal introduction on the first day of our Whitman studies, two female seniors were madly scribbling notes to one another. With a frown, but really out of curiosity, I walked over to read what one had written: "I have these experiences *all the time!*" Her friend had responded enthusiastically in the affirmative. Indeed, adolescence brings with it the development of the ability to entertain abstract concepts of a sophisticated nature, making Whitman, the self-described "poet of the body and the soul," a perfect companion.

There are higher levels of spirituality in poetry than the writings of Whitman—the poems of William Blake or Hindu texts like the *Bhagavad-Gita*—but at present these seem out of my own teaching range despite my absorption in them. What Whitman seemed to have experienced, however, was far more profound than my own little moments of transport. What especially appealed to me was Whitman's directness, the sense that he was speaking from the heart of a great mystery in a language that I could understand. Neither I nor my students need to cut through a lot of cultural differences and symbol-systems to understand Whitman, and this is what I wanted to explore and to communicate to them: an apprehension of spiritual matters that was immediate. Not that everything in his work can be understood; the studies of what Whitman meant in "Song of Myself" are still tumbling off the presses. I simply wanted the excuse at least to touch on spiritual things, and Whitman supplied the occasion.

Of course, all poetry is spiritual to a greater or lesser extent. Whitman himself wrote:

Much is said of what is spiritual, and of spirituality, in this, that, or the other—in objects, expressions.—For me, I see no object, no expression, no animal, no tree, no art, no book, but I see, from morning to night, and from night to morning, the spiritual.—Bodies are all spiritual.—All words are spiritual—nothing is more spiritual than words. (*An American Primer*, p. 1)

In Class

After I had told the story of my youthful "experiences" and read aloud the passages from "Song of Myself" quoted in the first item of the following list, my classes and I used the chalkboard to make a grand list of the features that seemed to be characteristic of Whitman's poems. (My seniors had already read "Song of Myself," "The Sleepers," "Faces," and "I Sing the Body Electric" from the 1855 text of *Leaves of Grass*; my sophomores read the final edition of the "Song" and "Out of the Cradle Endlessly Rocking" in *The Mentor Book of Major American Poets*.) Here's our list:

1. *Spirituality*: By which is meant an appeal to or manifestation of transcendence; an understanding that each individual is identical with the One. Everywhere in his work, but most notably in "Song of Myself," Whitman refers to the central fact of his life, the spiritual experience which he evidently had sometime in the early 1850s, first memorialized in section 5 of the poem:

I believe in you my soul . . . . the other I am must not abase itself to you,
And you must not be abased to the other.
. . .
I mind how we lay in June, such a transparent summer morning;
You settled your head athwart my hips and gently turned over upon me,
And parted the shirt from my bosom-bone, and plunged your tongue to
    my barestript heart,
And reached till you felt my beard, and reached till you held my feet.

Swiftly arose and spread around me the peace and joy and knowledge
    that pass all the art and argument of the earth;
And I know that the hand of God is the elderhand of my own,
And I know that the spirit of God is the eldest brother of my own,
And that all the men ever born are also my brothers . . . . and the women
    my sisters and lovers,
And that a kelson of the creation is love;
And limitless are leaves stiff or drooping in the fields,
And brown ants in the little wells beneath them,
And mossy scabs of the wormfence, and heaped stones, and elder and
    mullein and poke-weed. (ll. 73–74, 78–89)

And in section 7 he returns to it:

Has any one supposed it lucky to be born?
I hasten to inform him or her it is just as lucky to die, and I know it.
I pass death with the dying, and birth with the new-washed babe . . . .
    and am not contained between my hat and boots.
And peruse manifold objects, no two alike, and every one good,
The earth good, and the stars good, and their adjuncts all good.

I am not an earth nor an adjunct of an earth,
I am the mate and companion of people, all just as immortal and
    fathomless as myself;
They do not know how immortal, but I know. (ll. 122–129)

The erotic language of the first description is perfectly
consistent with the narratives of saints and mystics. (One thinks
of Saint Theresa's account of being pierced with a spear by an
angel. We examined a picture of Bernini's famous statue for a
better understanding of what Whitman is "about" in this passage.)

Another technique that Whitman uses to generate the feeling
of "eternity" in many of his greatest poems is to keep to the
present tense. In "Song of Myself" one must search far and wide
for any use of the past tense.

2. *Emphasis on the physical body*: That the body is good,
clean, pure, etc.

3. *Celebration/praise*: All of creation is good and worthy of
praise. Kenneth Koch and Kate Farrell mention that the "Song
of Myself" is an "exuberant inventory of the world (and so of Walt
Whitman) in which he congratulates and praises all the parts of
life in great detail, and all for just existing." (*Sleeping on the Wing*,
p. 37)

4. *Love for all things*: "good" or "evil"—a repudiation of du-
ality, which is merely the misreading of a unified principle, since
the unenlightened human mind is incapable of grasping the
One. Furthermore, the compassion that we find everywhere
expressed in Whitman's writing may be seen as a form of
imagination, allowing us to feel what others are feeling.

5. *Equality*: of all humans; also, there is more than a hint in
Whitman that the processes of nature exist on a par with human
life. Section 32 begins, "I think I could turn and live awhile with
the animals . . . . they are so placid and self contained, / I stand
and look at them sometimes half the day long." (ll. 684–685)

6. *The list or catalog*: That Whitman's lists "level" every-

thing, thus making everything equal. This is to say that finally, in his lists, nothing takes precedence over another thing, and nothing comes first or last. The notion of the democratic—another key idea in Whitman's work—abides in such a conception.

7. *The simultaneity of the list*: Chains of events happening at once, which leads to a feeling of timelessness. The poet is thus godlike, standing at the center of time, able to see and feel all things at once. Also, the poet tends to disappear into his enumerations, a technique that increases the feeling of spirituality, of Oneness, the detachment from ego. Simultaneity also creates a sense of movement, often of speed, in the text.

8. *Repetition*: A phenomenon of the list. It creates an incantatory feeling, as in religious literature, that approaches the rhythms of the prayer or chant, heightening the sense of the spiritual. A discussion of Whitman's use of rhetorical devices such as anaphora (the repetition of the same word or words at the *beginning* of a line), epistrophe (the repetition of the same word or words at the *end* of a line), symploce (the combination of anaphora and epistrophe), and syntactical parallelism can sharpen the students' understanding of Whitman's poetic technique. These devices literally "make" his meaning.

9. *Highly physical description alternating with abstract spiritual musings*: Whitman gains a tremendous power in his work because he continually buttresses his spiritual insights with concrete particulars (observed facts), and vice versa.

10. *Sexuality*: Whitman does not shy away from expressions of sexuality; this connects several of the above categories in our list—spirituality, equality, democracy, physical description, love, celebration, and, of course, eroticism.

11. *Intimacy of address*: The voice of Whitman is warm, friendly, encouraging, sometimes even animated by the fearlessness found in face-to-face conversation. He addresses the reader directly, creating a sense of closeness rare in poetry.

12. *Individuality*: Despite the tendency of catalog poetry to "dissolve" the author's identity, his or her individual personality persists by virtue of the literary choices made and style adopted. (The students and I were forced to acknowledge a paradoxical element here: to know that one is an individual and at the same time one with the Whole.)

13. *Fearless use of the first person pronoun*: Whitman never shies away from using the word "I." "Song of Myself" begins with

it ("I celebrate myself") and virtually ends with it ("I stop some where waiting for you"). The constant use of the *I* is another element that creates the instantaneous intimacy of Whitman's voice.

14. *"And to die is different from what any one supposed, and luckier"*: This line concludes and summarizes section 6, which begins with the famous opening, "A child said, What is the grass? fetching it to me with full hands." (6.1) The realization of individual death is transcended by the understanding that the soul is immortal.

15. *Natural diction spiced with 'poetic' diction*: Whitman's sound—his choice of words—is very close to ours, very "modern." The "everydayness" of his vocabulary reflects the common sights and sounds that he celebrates. Whitman's language is also highly concrete and sensual, as if it could be grabbed and held before the eyes and felt with the hand. At the same time, we note that his use of certain words and expressions (sometimes from the French, especially in the poems after 1855) may be a bit off-putting: "venerealee" for one afflicted with venereal disease; "amies" for "female friends"; "chef-d'oeuvre" for "masterpiece"; "ambulanza" for "ambulance"; "eleves" for "students"; "bussing" for "kissing," etc.

16. *A poet of the city*: Whitman was the first great poet to write of New York City, which connects to

17. *The poet as reporter*: For many years Whitman worked as a newspaperman. He went out into the streets, using his eyes and ears to gather facts—sights, sounds, smells, textures—that informed his writing. This technique was to lay the foundation for everything that he would write. In short, observation—the merging of one's sensibility with one's surroundings—is another way of being-at-one with the "other." It is a form of meditation, and thus intersects with many of these other categories.

18. *The poet as storyteller*: There are anecdotes and short narratives throughout Whitman's long poems, especially in "Song of Myself," even though this poem is thought of as a non-narrative work. "[T]he subject was so large that anything, it seemed, could be part of it and could be included." (Koch and Farrell, *Sleeping on the Wing*, p. 37)

19. *Frequent and unusual use of the ellipsis (. . . .)*: Particularly odd in nineteenth-century poetry. This piece of punctuation is Whitman's hieroglyph for the drawn breath, the pause for

thought, the opening-up of the poem into timelessness, the intrusion of the eternal into consciousness whenever we leave off speaking—that is, when the individual ego is adumbrated. At the end of a poem the ellipsis usually means something like, "I have nothing more to say." In Whitman it means something different: a unit of breath; little stars or planets rolling by. . . .

20. *The long line*: Whitman's long lines contain or generate many of the above qualities. His line is a rolling wave, an oceanic motion; a planetary orbit; the process of drawing and exhaling breath—as a focus in meditation. (The long line also testifies to Whitman's devotion to opera.)

The origin of Whitman's line in Biblical literature seems evident. Here is a passage from the Old Testament (which I have arranged into verse lines) that contains the seed of Whitman's major theme in "Song of Myself":

Comfort ye, comfort ye my people, saith your God.
Speak ye comfortably to Jerusalem, and cry unto her, that her warfare
   is accomplished, that her iniquity is pardoned: for she hath received
   of the Lord's hand double for all her sins.
The voice of him that crieth in the wilderness,
Prepare ye the way of the Lord, make straight in the desert a highway
   for our God.
Every valley shall be exalted, and every mountain and hill shall be
   made low: and the crooked shall be made straight, and the rough
   places plain:
And the glory of the Lord shall be revealed, and all flesh shall see it
   together: for the mouth of the Lord hath spoken it.
The voice said, Cry. And he said, What shall I cry? All flesh is grass, and
   all the goodliness thereof is as the flower of the field:
The grass withereth, the flower fadeth: because the spirit of the Lord
   bloweth upon it: surely the people is grass.
The grass withereth, the flower fadeth: but the word of our God shall
   stand for ever. (Isaiah 40:1–8, King James Version)

The voice of God speaks through the mouth of the prophet, and Whitman himself for a time thought of his book as a "new Bible" for the American masses. Grass recurs as a life-image throughout literature and mythology. The Oglala Sioux holy man Black Elk, at the beginning of his autobiography, says: "So many other men have lived and shall live that story (of an individual life), to be grass upon the hills" (*Black Elk*

Speaks, p. 1). We grow, flourish, and die like blades of grass. Whitman's title suggests the leaves (pages) of a book, at once eternal and transitory. We can also imagine a book printed on blades of grass, each blade being the page of the book of eternity. Guy Davenport notes that "this one universal plant [is] absent only in the deserts of the poles," and that "the first paper was leaves of grass, papyrus" (Davenport, p. 76). Hence Whitman's description of it as a "uniform hieroglyphic." Grass, tenacious and ubiquitous, is also a perfect symbol for democracy. (Again note that Whitman's image is oxymoronic: grass that may need deciphering, but also is universal, accessible to all.)

Naturally there is much more to be said on all these subjects, and there are plenty of insights attendant on a close reading of Whitman. My students and I arrived at these ideas in a class session of "brainstorming," and I offer them as points of departure for further discussion. Use them as best suits your purpose.

Imitating Whitman

My students wrote imitations of Whitman using our list of twenty characteristics, trying to include in their poems as many of them as possible. If students had experienced "cosmic" moments that my personal introduction or Whitman's poetry reminded them of, or that Whitman's poems revived, I urged them to include these moments in their poems, and to be as specific as possible.

Whitman's poems give the feeling of being *in* reality, so I took the students outside to a little community park in our neighborhood where all of us could sit and write. This exercise proved useful to students who found it difficult to identify with the spiritual aspect of Whitman's poetry; direct observation gave them images and events to "hang on to." Thus a "Whitman imitation" can also be a transcription of reality—a meditation on what passes before the eye and ear. These observations could be written down in prose, then later arranged into Whitmanic verse lines. (According to biographer Paul Zweig, Whitman ultimately found his poetic voice through years of writing prose—everything from newspaper articles to journal entries. His early poetry is mediocre, at best.) Here's a first draft of my foray into the garden:

Small apartment buildings being built in the air around us.
I watch the workers in yellow helmets and heavy-soled boots walk the
   rooftops, banging and buzzing away, shouting and laughing.
An airplane flies over. What am I thinking?
Strands of cassette tape festoon a nearby tree.
I sit on a bench in the garden planted with dozens of blossoming flowers
   and shrubs,
alive with immense bees that flash in and out of the Indian summer
   sunlight, strong because of the clearness of the air.
Small gnats attracted to skinny black trees attack my face as I write.
I puff my cheeks and whoosh, they go spinning upwards!
There is the shadow-work of these little trees to try to get down in words,
   the twisted puppet patterns thrown on the white-washed brick sides
   of adjacent brownstones.
The shadows remind me of the black ink that unrolls from the tip of my
   black pen, shiny in the sunlight.
Tiny suns race up and down its barrel like meteorites!

I look at the students as they write, ranged in odd or formal positions
   around the circular garden, scribbling in our notebooks, and think
   about making a list of what each of us is doing.
Are they sneaking looks at me, too, I wonder, as I note this down?
Alton creeps near some bushes, training his ever-ready camera on a
   black cat that has suddenly appeared.
Half of us are watching him and madly trying to write it down.
Alison sits on a rock, crosslegged, staring her eyes down at her pad,
   looking like Buddha.
My pen is moving along the page—I can't stop writing!

Other observations—drawn from reality, from memory, or
from the imagination—can be interspersed with this "on-the-
spot writing." This new material may be of a philosophical or
cosmic nature, but should be balanced by the "minute particulars" captured for the pen by the eye and ear. The point is to let
abstract ideas be generated and controlled by concrete images,
and not the other way around: start with the skinny black tree
in the garden that a thousand gnats are whirling around and
then speak of the years that fly so quickly at Time's frozen face.
Then move back to another concrete image—the splotchy, neon-
like colors on the bow tie of the assistant principal, for example.
   It would also be a good idea to use some of the rhetorical

devices employed by Whitman that I mentioned in the eighth item of the list of qualities: anaphora, epistrophe, symploce, and syntactical parallelism. It's easy to find examples of these techniques in Whitman's poems.

If it isn't convenient to go outdoors, students can rely on remembered images. Writers can start with something that they know well—the trip to school in the morning, for example. They can "borrow" material from magazines and books if there is a danger of running out of steam. (News magazines and *National Geographic* are good sources of images.) In fact, if your school has a library, it might be the ideal place to do this kind of writing, as long as students aren't too distracted by the temptation to do nothing but browse through books and periodicals.

Once students have achieved a Whitmanic *flow* in their work, this kind of poem can keep going and going. It can be stocked with anecdotes and little stories, as well as fleeting descriptions. It can be broken into sections that are more or less self-contained, or ones that spill over into the next section.

Study the endings of Whitman's poems and you will note that they often simply trail off, or end rather abruptly, even arbitrarily; many of them might end anywhere. The impressions simply stop coming, or in some way cease, as if the poet decided to step out of the river of being that created the images. This quality, too, is a mark of Whitman's work, or of the kind of poem that records a stretch of mental time in which anything might happen. Some critics have felt that Whitman's writing is a sort of stream-of-consciousness or free-association technique. Here too the spiritual is invoked: the feeling that one is centered in one's body and in no need of heading anywhere. One *is*, and whatever swims through the mind is registered, then let go of. That is how students might learn to think of this kind of writing: grab the image, get it down, then be ready for the next image. What unifies the perception of these images is the mind—and, in the largest sense, the Mind that watches over the whole universe; which *is* the universe.

A Polemical Aside

I have before me three poetry textbooks used in high school and college. Two of these texts, which incidentally feature substantial anthologies that "fill out" the books, offer poems by Walt Whitman. The first book (532 pages) reprints six Whitman poems, none of which is longer than twenty-four lines (the average poem is thirteen lines long): "Beat! Beat! Drums!," "Cavalry Crossing a Ford," "I Saw in Louisiana a Live-Oak Growing," "A Noiseless Patient Spider," "O Captain! My Captain!," and "The Runner." An additional snippet, ten lines from "Song of Myself," introduces the book's anthology section. In all, the book contains eighty-nine lines of Whitman's poetry.

The other anthology—564 pages—does much better: "Out of the Cradle Endlessly Rocking," certainly one of Whitman's greatest poems (183 lines); "When I Heard the Learn'd Astronomer"; "Cavalry Crossing a Ford"; "When Lilacs Last in the Dooryard Bloom'd," the Lincoln elegy that is far superior to "O Captain! My Captain!" (and a poem of 206 lines); "A Noiseless Patient Spider"; and "The Dalliance of the Eagles." Average: 70.6 lines per poem, though the four short poems here are ten lines or fewer. At least, we are given a sense of Whitman's *heft* as a poet in the longer works.

For comparison I went to a widely used poetry text currently in its seventh edition. It contained five poems by Whitman—"A Noiseless Patient Spider," "Come Up from the Fields Father," "Had I the Choice," "There Was a Child Went Forth" (the "heavyweight" here, at thirty-nine lines), and "When I Heard the Learn'd Astronomer." Total: 103 lines of Whitman; average poem: 20.6 lines.

It doesn't take a statistical genius to see that, if indeed Whitman is one of our nation's major poets (and he is), and if he is one of the great poets of the world (a universally acknowledged fact), we are being shortchanged in the quantity (not to mention the quality) of his work that is being offered to our students. A quick tally shows *what* of Whitman gets anthologized—poems ten lines or under that don't pack much of a punch or don't contain much of Whitman's philosophy. They are imagistic sketches, not even vignettes, and in them the poet simply does not have the opportunity to do what he does best—stretch out and soar. Of "O Captain! My Captain!," perhaps the most anthologized Whitman poem, biographer Justin Kaplan has reported:

Sometimes [Whitman] regretted ever having written it. ("It's My Captain again; always My Captain," he exclaimed when the Harper publishing house asked his permission to print it in a school reader. "My God! when will they listen to me for whole and good?" If this was his "best," he said, "what can the worst be like?") (*Walt Whitman: A Life,* p. 29)

It is on that great long poem that came to be called "Song of Myself," in its 1855 incarnation of 1,336 lines (before Whitman tinkered with it in later editions of *Leaves of Grass*), that Whitman's reputation chiefly rests—or ought to. (Other works in the 1855 edition are also great: certainly "The Sleepers" and "Faces," and perhaps "I Sing the Body Electric.") The later "Out of the Cradle Endlessly Rocking," "When Lilacs Last in the Dooryard Bloom'd," and "Crossing Brooklyn Ferry" are also great and substantial poems. Some of the erotic poems in the "Calamus" section of the *Leaves* are powerful, as are a few of the Civil War poems in the "Drum Taps" section. Also worth study are the various poems with "Song" in their titles, a grouping that includes "Salut au Monde!" and "Our Old Feuillage."

Why not take Whitman at his word? If students can read 300-page novels, surely they can read a hundred pages of his best work.

Additional Writing Ideas

For academic or research papers, students could explore some of the following ideas:

• *Whitman and the Spiritual*: A good introduction to the mystical tradition may be found in *The Perennial Philosophy* by Aldous Huxley (New York: Harper & Row, 1970; first published 1945). *Cosmic Consciousness* by Whitman's disciple, Dr. R. M. Bucke, was praised by the poet, who claimed that "it thoroughly delineates me" (Kaplan, pp. 37–38). The psychologist William James's *The Varieties of Religious Experience* (New York: New American Library) was originally published in 1902 and contains a good deal of material on Whitman. The connection between the metaphysics of Hinduism and Whitman can be probed in "Whitman and Indian Thought" by V. K. Chari (found in Bradley and Blodgett) and in Chari's book, *Whitman in the Light of Vedantic Mysticism—An Interpretation* (Lincoln, NE: University of Nebraska Press, 1964). For a contrast to Whitman's view of the One in a poem like "Song of Myself" see "The Eleventh Teaching: The Vision of Krishna's Totality" in *The Bhagavad-Gita: Krishna's Counsel in Time of War,* translated by Barbara Stoler Miller (New York: Bantam Books, 1986), which keeps the verse form of the original. Transcendentalism, the sociophilosophical movement of the nineteenth century that had a powerful impact on Whitman, may be scrutinized in *The Transcendentalists: An Anthology*, edited by Perry Miller (Cambridge: Harvard University Press, 1950). See also *Transcendentalism in New England: A History* by Octavius Brooks Frothingham (Gloucester, MA: Peter Smith, 1965; originally published 1876) and, for short articles, *The Transcendentalist Revolt Against Materialism*, edited with an introduction by George F. Whicher (Boston: D. C. Heath & Co., 1949). The biographies of Whitman and Gay Wilson Allen's biography of Emerson also look into the relationship between Whitman and Transcendentalist thought.

• *"Walking Around" Poetry*: Whitman is one of a number of poets who have written poems "on foot" (or who creates the illusion of doing so). For other masters of this genre, see work by Guillaume Apollinaire (in translations from the French), Charles Reznikoff, and Frank O'Hara. The "walking around" poem is predominantly a city genre, so it is no surprise that all of these poets (and there are others) lived in New York or Paris.

• *Poems on the Assassination of Abraham Lincoln*: Not surprisingly, many poets besides Whitman wrote tributes when Lincoln was murdered. Some of them were collected in *Poems of American History*, edited by Burton Egbert Stevenson (Boston: Houghton Mifflin, 1922), pp. 537–544. To find this fascinating book, long out of print, you will have to hunt it down in libraries, but the search is worth it. Students can compare other elegies to Whitman's "O Captain! My Captain!" and "When Lilacs Last in the Dooryard Bloom'd." The assignment could be extended to compare the reaction of poets to John F. Kennedy's assassination in *Of Poetry and Power* (New York: Basic Books, 1964).

• *Emerson and Whitman*: For many years the poet and great essayist Ralph Waldo Emerson beat the drum for a new kind of American poetry. Whitman was quite familiar with Emerson's essays and lectures and with the chief ideas of the Transcendentalist movement "fathered" by Emerson. (When Whitman sent him a copy of *Leaves of Grass* in 1855, Emerson wrote back to say that Whitman's book was "the most extraordinary piece of wit & wisdom that America has yet contributed" (Kaplan, pp. 202–203). Students could read Emerson's essays "The Transcendentalist" and "The Poet" (see Emerson's *Selected Essays*, edited by Larzer Ziff [New York: Penguin Books, 1982]) to search for his ideas about the new American poet, and see how applicable they are to Whitman. The most recent biography of Emerson, *Waldo Emerson: A Biography* by Gay Wilson Allen (New York: Viking Press, 1981), should also be consulted. Allen has also published a standard Whitman biography, and knows the intellectual terrain of this period.

• *Contemporaries and Followers of Whitman*: Older poetry anthologies and histories of American poetry (such as *A Short History of American Poetry* by Donald Barlow Stauffer [New York: E. P. Dutton, 1974]) contain interesting selections from and commentaries on the poetry of Whitman's contemporaries. Beginning with Emerson, students could compare and contrast the writings of various poets to those of Whitman: William Gilmore Simms (1806–1870); Henry Wadsworth Longfellow (1807–1882); John Greenleaf Whittier (1807–1892); Edgar Allan Poe (1809–1849); Oliver Wendell Holmes (1809–1894); Christopher Pearse Cranch (1813–1872), whose use of a long, prosaic line may have influenced Whitman; Jones Very (1813–1880); Henry David Thoreau (1817–1862); Herman Melville and James Russell Lowell (both 1819–1891), born the same year as Whitman, who outlived them by one year; Frederick Goddard Tuckerman (1821–1873); and Bayard Taylor (1825–1878).

Whitman disciples whose work could be examined include Edward Carpenter (1844–1929) and Carl Sandburg (1878–1967).

• *Whitman's Poetic Language*: In the foreword to *An American Primer*, Whitman said: "I sometimes think that the *Leaves* is only a language experiment." Using *An American Primer* as a guide, students could put Whitman's language "under the microscope," studying what makes it visceral and what gives it its spiritual quality. What are his favorite words? From what sources does he derive his vocabulary? The same could be done for his rhetorical devices—anaphora, epistrophe, etc.

• *Whitman's Prose Works:* Whitman's prefaces to his various editions of *Leaves of Grass* repay close reading. Students will find them collected in Bradley and Blodgett. *An American Primer* is a delightful excursion into the American language, and could be updated by students to include current slang and catch-phrases. Students could also write their own *Specimen Days.* Other prose works, including short fiction and a novel, have been published in the monumental *Collected Writings of Walt Whitman*, currently being issued by New York University Press.

How the Poets See Whitman: A Little Survey

Many poets have responded to *Leaves of Grass* with tributes of their own. Students can do reports on some of the poets who have been influenced by him or who have answered him in their own work. The poets listed below represent a small sampling of these responses.

The first poets of reputation to be influenced by Whitman were French. Jules Laforgue translated parts of *Leaves of Grass* into French and experimented with Whitman's long free verse line. Early in the twentieth century Valery Larbaud wrote travelogue-type poems about the "open road" so dear to Whitman. In Portugal, Fernando Pessoa invented a wonderfully crazy "Salutation to Walt Whitman" that sounds like T. S. Eliot's timid J. Alfred Prufrock going wild after reading "Song of Myself." (Pessoa was educated in England and quite familiar with Whitman's poems, since the American poet had admirers among the English poets—including Swinburne, Tennyson, and Hopkins—long before his work became popular in the United States.) In the 1920s and 1930s, writers like Sherwood Anderson (who wrote poetry as well as fiction) and Carl Sandburg were deeply influenced by Whitman. Hart Crane dedicated a section of his long poem "The Bridge" to Whitman, ending it: "My hand / in yours, / Walt Whitman—/ so—" D. H. Lawrence, best known for his novels, used Whitman's long line in some of his greatest poems, including "Snake" and "Bavarian Gentians." Federico García Lorca, visiting the United States in 1929–1930, wrote an "Ode to Walt Whitman" that appeared in his book *Poet in New York.* Langston Hughes wrote, "I, too, sing America. // I am the darker brother," in one of his most famous poems, and many of his other poems show that he had carefully read his Whitman. The Chilean poet Pablo Neruda showed Whitman's influence

especially in his long poem *Residence on Earth*. Neruda had this
to say in an address given in New York City in 1972:

I was barely fifteen when I discovered Walt Whitman, my primary
creditor. I stand here among you today still owing this marvelous debt
that has helped me live.

To renegotiate this debt is to begin by making it public, by proclaiming
myself the humble servant of the poet who measured the earth with
long, slow strides, pausing everywhere to love and to examine, to learn,
to teach, and to admire. That man, that lyric moralist, chose a difficult
road; he was a torrential and didactic bard. These two qualities seem
antithetical, more appropriate for a caudillo than for a writer. But what
really matters is that the professor's chair, teaching, the apprenticeship
to life held no fear for Walt Whitman, and he accepted the responsibility
of teaching with candor and eloquence. Clearly, he feared neither
morality nor immorality, nor did he attempt to define the boundaries
between pure and impure poetry. He is the first absolute poet, and it was
his intention not only to sing but to impart his vast vision of the
relationships of men and of nations. In this sense, his obvious nation-
alism is part of an organic universality. He considers himself indebted
to happiness and sorrow, to advanced cultures and primitive societies.

Greatness has many faces, but I, a poet who writes in Spanish,
learned more from Walt Whitman than from Cervantes. In Whitman's
poetry the ignorant are never humbled, and the human condition is
never derided.

We are still living in a Whitmanesque epoch; in spite of painful birth
pangs, we are witnessing the emergence of new men and new societies.
The bard complained of the all-powerful European influence that
continued to dominate the literature of his time. In fact, it was he, Walt
Whitman, in the persona of a specific geography, who for the first time
in history brought honor to an American name. The colonialism of the
most brilliant nations created centuries of silence; in three centuries of
Spanish domination we had no more than two or three outstanding
writers in all America. (*Passions and Impressions*, pp. 376–377)

William Carlos Williams asserted that Keats and Whitman
were the first two poets to make their mark on him. His
judgment of Whitman was divided. On the one hand, Whitman
broke new ground by his use of the American vernacular, a
development that Williams thoroughly approved of and followed
in his own poetic practice. On the other hand, Williams felt that
Whitman didn't know what to do with the free verse he had
invented:

Whitman to me was an instrument, one thing: he started us on the course of our researches into the nature of the line by breaking finally with English prosody. After him there has been for us no line. There will be none until we invent it. Almost everything I do is of no more interest to me than the technical addition it makes toward the discovery of a workable metric in the new mode. (*The Selected Letters of William Carlos Williams,* pp. 286–287)

Eleven years later, in 1961, Williams told an interviewer that "Whitman's line is too long for the modern poet. At the present time I have been trying to approach a shorter line which I haven't quite been able to nail." This line would be "more terse, and absolutely not the stretching out of the line that Whitman did" (*Interviews with William Carlos Williams,* p. 39). Interestingly enough, Williams told his interviewer: "I don't hear any Biblical form in [Whitman's] poems" (*ibid.,* p. 42).

Poet Allen Ginsberg has proven to be Whitman's most outspoken contemporary champion, though Ginsberg's long line was also shaped by the unrhymed poems of William Blake. In an interview, Ginsberg remembered his days as a college student at Columbia (in the 1940s) and the attitude towards Whitman that prevailed:

He was taught but he was much insulted. I remember, around the time of the writing of *On the Road* [by Jack Kerouac], a young favored instructor at Columbia College told me that Whitman was not a serious writer because he had no discipline and William Carlos Williams was an awkward provincial, no craft, and Shelley was a sort of silly fool! So there was no genuine professional poetics taught at Columbia, there was a complete obliteration and amnesia of the entire great mind of gnostic western philosophy or Hindu Buddhist eastern philosophy, no acceptance or conception of a possibility of a cosmic consciousness as a day to day experience or motivation or even once in a lifetime experience. It was all considered as some sort of cranky pathology. So Whitman was put down as a "negativist crude yea-sayer who probably had a frustrated homosexual libido and so was generalizing his pathology into oceanic consciousness of a morbid nature which had nothing to do with the real task of real men in a real world surrounded by dangerous communist enemies" [laughs] or something like that. (*Composed on the Tongue,* pp. 69–70)

Ginsberg adapted the rhythm of his poem "Howl" (1956) in part from the anaphora-laden "Song of Myself." The long line was also employed in "Kaddish" (1961), the deeply moving elegy for his mother, and in his tribute to Whitman, "In a Supermarket in California":

What thoughts I have of you tonight, Walt Whitman, for I walked down the sidestreets under the trees with a headache self-conscious looking at the full moon.
In my hungry fatigue, and shopping for images, I went into the neon fruit supermarket, dreaming of your enumerations!
What peaches and what penumbras! Whole families shopping at night! Aisles full of husbands! Wives in the avocados, babies in the tomatoes! — and you, Garcia Lorca, what were you doing down by the watermelons? (*Howl and Other Poems*, p. 23)

Louis Simpson carried on an argument with Whitman's prophetic poems ("Song of the Redwoods," "Song of the Open Road") in his book called *At the End of the Open Road* (1963). His "Walt Whitman at Bear Mountain" challenges the optimistic view of America and the faith in progress that came to be major Whitman themes. Its first stanzas read:

Neither on horseback nor seated,
But like himself, squarely on two feet,
The poet of death and lilacs
Loafs by the footpath. Even the bronze looks alive
Where it is folded like cloth. And he seems friendly.

"Where is the Mississippi panorama
And the girl who played the piano?
Where are you, Walt?
The Open Road goes to the used car lot.

"Where is the nation you promised?
These houses built of wood sustain
Colossal snows,
And the light above the street is sick to death.

"As for the people—see how they neglect you!
Only a poet pauses to read the inscription."

Simpson has some superb observations as well as penetrating criticisms to make of Whitman:

Whitman's "philosophy" . . . consists of two or three ideas. One, it is possible to merge in your feelings with others, and it is possible for others to merge in their feelings with you. Two, if this occurs over a distance, or over a span of time, it seems to annihilate space and time. This is a kind of immortality. Three, in order to convey your feelings to others you must, by a process of empathic observation, using all your senses, take things into yourself and express them again. The senses are "dumb ministers" of feeling . . . through them we know one another. The poet is the manager of this process—he puts what we feel and see into words. (*Selected Prose*, p. 322)

Some other poets who have adopted Whitman's long line for their own use include Robinson Jeffers, Kenneth Fearing, the Italian writer Cesare Pavese, and Kenneth Koch, whose poem "Faces" (which focuses on the same theme as the Whitman poem of 1855 that was eventually given this title) shows the hallmark Whitmanic anaphora:

The face of the gypsy watching the bird gun firing into the colony of
    seals; but it was filled with blanks;
The face of the old knoll watching his hills grow up before him;
The face of the New England fruit juice proprietor watching his whole
    supplies being overturned by a herd of wild bulls;
The face of a lemur watching the other primates become more developed;
The face of gold, as the entire world goes on the silver standard, but gold
    remains extremely valuable and is the basis for international ex-
    change;
The face of the sky, as the air becomes increasingly filled with smoke
    and planes;
The face of the young girl painted as Saint Urbana by Perugino, whose
    large silver eyes are focused on the green pomegranate held by a baby
    (it is Jesus) in the same painting;
The face of the sea after there has been a storm, and the face of the valley
When the clouds have blown away and it is going to be a pleasant day
    and the pencils come out for their picnic;
The face of the clouds . . .
                                        (*The Pleasures of Peace*, p. 86)

Charles Reznikoff was perhaps the greatest poet of New York City after Whitman. His street scenes and mininarratives also employ the long line and focus on the experiences of ordinary people:

She sat by the window opening into the airshaft,
and looked across the parapet
at the new moon.

She would have taken the hairpins out of her carefully coiled hair,
and thrown herself on the bed in tears;
but he was coming and her mouth had to be pinned into a smile.
If he would have her, she would marry whatever he was.

A knock. She lit the gas and opened her door.
Her aunt and the man—skin loose under his eyes, the face slashed with
    wrinkles.
"Come in," she said as gently as she could and smiled.

(Complete Poems, p. 32)

In "Musical Shuttle," Harvey Shapiro remembers his youthful
reading of Whitman's "Out of the Cradle Endlessly Rocking."
Both poems are about the origins of the impulse to write poetry,
which Whitman says came to him "Out of the mocking-bird's
throat, the musical shuttle," as he watched the mating of two
birds near the Long Island surf. Shapiro also finds himself on the
Long Island shore:

[. . .]
I walked the shore
Where cold rocks mourned in water
Like the planets lost in air.
Ocean was a low sound.
The gate-keeper suddenly gone,
Whatever the heart cried
Voice tied to dark sound.
The shuttle went way back then,
Hooking me up to the first song
That ever chimed in my head.
Under a sky gone slick with stars,
The aria tumbling forth:
Bird and star . . .

(National Cold Storage Company, p. 52)

Whitman's followers are by now, of course, legion. His long
line has passed into the public domain, where any poet can pick
it up and bend it to his or her needs. That so many writers have

done it constitutes yet another tribute to Whitman's genius. What we ought to remember is that Whitman forged his poetics in his own way. This, more than any tradition, seems to be the path for the American writer. If we use Walt Whitman as a guide, it ought to be to help us towards our own originality.

•

Bibliography

I. References for This Article

A. BOOKS AND ARTICLES

Ginsberg, Allen. *Composed on the Tongue*. Edited by Donald Allen (Bolinas, CA: Grey Fox Press, 1979). Interviews and essays by Ginsberg.

Koch, Kenneth, and Kate Farrell. *Sleeping on the Wing: An Anthology of Modern Poetry with Essays on Reading and Writing* (New York: Random House, 1981; Vintage Books, 1982).

Neihardt, John G. *Black Elk Speaks: Being the Life Story of a Holy Man of the Oglala Sioux* (Lincoln, NE: University of Nebraska Press, 1961; originally published in 1932).

Neruda, Pablo. *Passions and Impressions*. Edited by Matilde Neruda and Miguel Otero Silva, translated by Margaret Sayers Peden (New York: Farrar, Straus & Giroux, 1983).

Simpson, Louis. *Selected Prose* (New York: Paragon House, 1989).

Wagner, Linda Welshimer, ed. *Interviews with William Carlos Williams: "Speaking Straight Ahead"* (New York: New Directions, 1976).

Whitman, Walt. The Malcolm Cowley edition of the 1855 *Leaves of Grass*. (See "Texts," below, for full bibliographical entry.)

_____. *An American Primer: With Facsimiles of the Original Manuscript*. Edited by Horace Traubel (San Francisco: City Lights Books, 1970; reprinted Duluth, MN: Holy Cow! Press, 1987; originally published in 1904).

Williams, William Carlos. *The Selected Letters of William Carlos Williams.* Edited with an introduction by John C. Thirlwall (New York: McDowell, Obolensky, 1957).

B. BOOKS OF POETRY

Crane, Hart. *The Complete Poems and Selected Letters and Prose.* Edited with an introduction and notes by Brom Weber (Garden City, NY: Doubleday & Co., 1966).

Ginsberg, Allen. *Howl and Other Poems.* Introduction by William Carlos Williams (San Francisco: City Lights Books, 1956).

Jeffers, Robinson. *The Selected Poetry* (New York: Random House, 1938).

Koch, Kenneth. *The Pleasures of Peace and Other Poems* (New York: Grove Press, 1969).

Larbaud, Valery. *The Poems of A. O. Barnabooth.* Translated by Ron Padgett and Bill Zavatsky (Tokyo: Mushinsha Ltd., 1977).

Lorca, Federico García. *Poet in New York.* Translated by Greg Simon and Steven F. White. Edited with an introduction and notes by Christopher Maurer (New York: Farrar, Straus & Giroux, 1988).

Neruda, Pablo. *Residence on Earth.* Translated from the Spanish by Donald D. Walsh (New York: New Directions, 1973).

Pavese, Cesare. *Hard Labor.* Translated from the Italian and with an introduction by William Arrowsmith (Baltimore and London: The Johns Hopkins University Press, 1979).

Pessoa, Fernando. *Selected Poems.* Translated by Edwin Honig with an introduction by Octavio Paz (Chicago: The Swallow Press, 1971).

Reznikoff, Charles. *The Complete Poems 1918–1975* (Santa Rosa, CA: Black Sparrow, 1989).

Shapiro, Harvey. *National Cold Storage Company: New and Selected Poems* (Middletown, CT: Wesleyan University Press, 1988).

Simpson, Louis. *At the End of the Open Road* (Middletown, CT: Wesleyan University Press, 1963).

Williams, William Carlos. *The Collected Poems, Volume I: 1909–1939.* Edited by A. Walton Litz and Christopher MacGowan (New York: New Directions, 1986).

_____. *The Collected Poems, Volume II: 1939–1962*. Edited by Christopher MacGowan (New York: New Directions, 1988).

II. Texts

Whitman, Walt. *An American Primer* (San Francisco: City Lights Books, 1970; republished Duluth, MN: Holy Cow! Press, 1987; originally published in 1904). First edited and issued by Whitman's disciple, Horace Traubel, in 1904, this never-completed meditation on language is one of Whitman's most delightful texts. It may be used as a starting point for further discussions of Whitman's use of language, and the nature of American English in general.

_____. *Leaves of Grass: The First (1855) Edition*. Edited, with an introduction, by Malcolm Cowley (New York: Penguin Books, 1986; originally published in 1959). Cowley's excellent introduction makes as much sense out of the "structure" of Whitman's amorphous "Song of Myself" as any critic has. The virtue of this edition is that it gives us, with line numbers, the texts of important Whitman poems in their first—and purest—state. Unfortunately there are no explanatory notes to the poems, and Viking Penguin should get on the ball and commission someone to write them. There are too many odd vocabulary words and idiosyncratic usages for a high school student (even a college student) to cut through.

_____. *The Complete Poems*. Edited by Francis Murphy. (New York: Penguin Books, 1975). A fine edition, if a bit bulky to handle. Murphy includes the 1855 text of "Song of Myself," and there are good notes to the poems. Also included are the 1855, 1856, 1872, and 1876 prefaces to the book.

_____. *Leaves of Grass: Authoritative Texts; Prefaces; Whitman on His Art; Criticism*. Edited by Sculley Bradley and Harold W. Blodgett (New York: W. W. Norton & Co., "Norton Critical Edition," 1973; originally published in 1965). An excellent resource volume, but for library consultation rather than high school classroom use. Includes all of Whitman's poetry that one would want to read—uncollected poems, unpublished poems, manuscript fragments. Whitman's pronouncements "On His Art" are here, as well as thirty critical essays and reviews. (One of them—an unsigned, laudatory review—is by Walt himself.)

Especially interesting is "Whitman and Indian Thought" by V. K. Chari, who notes that although "the absence of any established evidence that Whitman studied the Hindu books has remained a serious hurdle in Whitman research, . . . [in] the years during which *Leaves* was in the making there was a considerable vogue in America for Hindu religious ideas. . . ." (pp. 926–927)

III. Critical Biographies

Allen, Gay Wilson. *The Solitary Singer: A Critical Biography of Walt Whitman* (New York: Grove Press, 1955). Still the most thorough look at Whitman's life and career.

Kaplan, Justin. *Walt Whitman: A Life* (New York: Simon & Schuster, 1980). A highly readable "popular" biography, and the most recent. Kaplan's judgment about the nature of Whitman's spirituality is worth quoting: "Whitman was not a 'mystic.' Conversion, discipline, renunciation of the self, the body, and the world are alien to *Leaves of Grass*. . . . He had shared the experience of countless people, irreligious by common standards, who had flashes of illumination or ecstasy. . . . The rhythm of these experiences is sexual and urgent . . . and he invoked it and prolonged it through poetry. . . ." (p. 190). Be that as it may, Kaplan's very description points to the centrality of the "illumination or ecstasy" that Whitman experienced. Students might especially profit from a reading of chapters 8–9 (pp. 146–183), which describe the various sciences and pseudo-sciences of the age (such as phrenology) that had a profound effect on Whitman.

Zweig, Paul. *Walt Whitman: The Making of the Poet* (New York: Basic Books, 1984). Zweig carefully builds up the history of Whitman's development as a poet in this scrupulously researched and thoughtful book. He too dismisses any real "illumination": "Whitman's version of the peace that passeth all understanding is of the body and from the body. It expands like a gathering sexual storm and 'droops' like the subsidence of feeling after the sexual climax. [We] will never know whether Whitman experienced such a moment and became a poet because of it" (p. 254). Zweig's position is interesting because he himself has recounted his own search for enlightenment as a devotee of Swami Muktananda in his fascinating autobiographical book *Three Journeys*.

IV. ESSAYS

These essays can be read and reported on by high school students, or used in term papers. It is important to note that chief among Whitman's defenders have been poets like D. H. Lawrence, Donald Hall, Kenneth Rexroth, Randall Jarrell, Cesare Pavese, Karl Shapiro, Guy Davenport, and William Carlos Williams.

Davenport, Guy. "Whitman" in *The Geography of the Imagination: Forty Essays* (San Francisco: North Point Press, 1981). A beautifully written and insightful essay: "[Whitman] closed the widening distance between poet and audience. He talks to us face to face, so that our choice is between listening and turning away. And in turning away there is the uneasy feeling that we are turning our backs on the very stars and on ourselves" (p. 70). "Whitman's fond gaze was for grace that is unaware of itself; his constant pointing to beauty in common robust people was a discovery. Custom said that beauty was elsewhere" (p. 71).

Gross, Harvey. *Sound and Form in Modern Poetry: A Study of Prosody from Thomas Hardy to Robert Lowell* (Ann Arbor: University of Michigan Press, 1964). Contains a provocative study of Whitman's prosody, which Gross calls "formal and ceremonious. . . . His proper mode is not speech but invocation; not conversation, but chant and ceremony" (p. 84). He tells us that "Whitman's basic contribution was the substitution of syntax for meter as the controlling prosodic element in his poetry" (p. 85). The effect of the lines is a musical one, depending on devices such as syntactical parallelism, anaphora, and ellipsis. The danger is that "Whitman's nonmetrical prosody is as capable of doggerel as Poe's metronome" (p. 88).

Hall, Donald. "Whitman: The Invisible World" in *To Keep Moving: Essays 1959–1969* (Geneva, NY: Hobart & William Smith Colleges Press, in association with Seneca Review, 1980). "Many of Whitman's admirers . . . speak of his catalogues, his multiplication of *things*. Yet, the seen world hardly exists for him, because he spiritualizes everything." An excellent essay, originally written to introduce a selection of Whitman's verse to readers in Great Britain.

_____. "The Long Foreground of Walt Whitman" in *The Weather for Poetry: Essays, Reviews, and Notes on Poetry,*

1977-81 (Ann Arbor: University of Michigan Press, 1982). An excellent review of Justin Kaplan's Whitman biography.

Jarrell, Randall. "Some Lines from Whitman" in *Poetry and the Age* (New York: Random House Vintage Books, 1955; originally published 1953). A crucial essay in the rehabilitation of Whitman's reputation, focusing on this "poet of the greatest and oddest delicacy and originality and sensitivity, so far as words are concerned."

Lawrence, D. H. "Whitman" in *Studies in Classic American Literature* (New York: Penguin, 1964; originally published in 1923). A wonderfully cranky piece of creative griping, in which Lawrence takes Whitman to task for the loss of self exhibited in the American poet's passion for "merging." Lawrence links Whitman to faceless mass society, i.e., conformity. In brief, the wish to attain to Allness threatens Lawrence's ego. His thrashings-about are a delight to witness, especially in the light of his acknowledgment of Whitman as a "very great poet." This essay also appears in Bradley and Blodgett.

Marx, Leo, ed. *The Americanness of Walt Whitman* (Boston: D. C. Heath & Co., Problems in American Civilization series, 1960). The text of the 1891–92 edition of "Song of Myself," accompanied by essays from de Tocqueville, Edward Dowden, John Jay Chapman, George Santayana, Van Wyck Brooks, R. W. B. Lewis, and Richard Chase. Also here are Lawrence's and Jarrell's essays.

Miller, Edwin Haviland. *Walt Whitman's "Song of Myself": A Mosaic of Interpretations* (Iowa City: University of Iowa Press, 1989). A fascinating and very useful volume that moves through Whitman's long poem line by line, citing critical articles that offer interpretations and giving their sources. Included is the 1855 text of "Song of Myself" and an extensive bibliography.

Miller, James E., Karl Shapiro, and Bernice Slote. *Start with the Sun: Studies in the Whitman Tradition* (Lincoln, NB: University of Nebraska Press, 1960). Notable for Karl Shapiro's essay on "Cosmic Consciousness" and Miller's "The Poetics of the Cosmic Poem," this collection extends the Whitman tradition to the work of D. H. Lawrence, Hart Crane, Dylan Thomas, and Henry Miller. Shapiro's "The First White Aboriginal" also appears in this volume.

Padgett, Ron, ed., with Bill Zavatsky. "Free Verse" in *Poetic Forms* (New York: Teachers & Writers Collaborative, 1988).

This cassette interview (which appeared as part of the "Poetic Forms" series originally broadcast on WNYE in New York City) is a discussion of free verse, with reference to the history of the form and Whitman's practice.

Pavese, Cesare. "Interpretation of Walt Whitman, Poet" in *American Literature: Essays and Opinions,* translated with an introduction by Edwin Fussell (Berkeley, Los Angeles, and London: University of California Press, 1970). An engaging essay by this important Italian fiction writer and poet, whose own long-lined poems show the influence of Whitman's free verse. Also in Bradley and Blodgett.

Pearce, Roy Harvey, ed. *Whitman: A Collection of Critical Essays* (Englewood Cliffs, NJ: Prentice-Hall, 1962). An excellent collection of essays that contains the Lawrence essay as well as essays or book chapters by Pearce, William Carlos Williams, Ezra Pound, James Miller, Jr., F. O. Matthiessen, Charles Feidelson, Jr., R. W. B. Lewis, Richard Chase, and others.

Perlman, Jim, Ed Folsom, and Dan Campion, eds. *Walt Whitman: The Measure of His Song* (Minneapolis: Holy Cow! Press, 1981). This wonderful and massive (394 pages) collection of poems, letters, and essays ranges from 1855 to 1980 and gathers tributes from many poets of various cultures.

Rexroth, Kenneth. "Walt Whitman: *Leaves of Grass*" in *Classics Revisited* (New York: Avon Books Discus Edition, 1969). A fine essay in which Rexroth points out that, among the many great nineteenth-century writers who became "self-alienated outcasts," Whitman "successfully refused alienation" (p. 249).

——————————. *American Poetry in the Twentieth Century* (New York: The Seabury Press/Continuum Books, 1971). Whitman is "the only American poet who from his day to ours has been a major world writer and who has influenced writers in every language—from Rabindranath Tagore, Francis Jammes, Emile Verhaeren, or Blaise Cendrars to the contemporary Matabele poet, Raymond Kunene" (p. 18). The entire book is worth reading, both for Rexroth's fluent style and his brilliant observations.

Shapiro, Karl. "The First White Aboriginal" in *In Defense of Ignorance* (New York: Random House Vintage Books, 1965; originally published in 1960). Another important essay that contributed toward the rehabilitation of Whitman's reputation. Shapiro begins with a comparison of Whitman and D. H.

Lawrence, then settles down to delineate Whitman's philosophy: "He is the one mystical writer of any consequence America has produced, the most original religious thinker we have; the poet of the greatest achievement; the first profound innovator; the most accomplished artist as well—but nobody says this nowadays. For in the twentieth century Walt Whitman is almost completely shunned by his fellows. He has no audience, neither a general audience nor a literary clique. Official criticism ignores him completely; modern neo-classicism, as it calls itself, acknowledges him with embarrassment" (p. 188).

Zavatsky, Bill. "Free Verse" in *The Teachers & Writers Handbook of Poetic Forms*, edited by Ron Padgett (New York: Teachers & Writers Collaborative, 1987). A short essay on free verse, with an example chosen from "Song of Myself" and suggestions for further reading and writing.

Walt Whitman the Teacher

by Ron Padgett

A lot of people who read Whitman's poetry and see him as an inspired loafer are surprised to learn that at one point in his life he was a schoolteacher. Beginning in 1836, at the age of seventeen, Whitman taught in various country schools on Long Island for around four years. Such schools tended to be one-room, unheated, ramshackle buildings, attended only part of the year, some with teachers who were unqualified. Whitman himself had left school when he was eleven. (One of his teachers later described him as "a big, good-natured lad, clumsy and slovenly in appearance, but not otherwise remarkable.") In one school, Whitman was paid $72.20 and board for a little more than five months' work, and the only holidays were Sundays and every other Saturday afternoon.

He differed from most of his colleagues in that he didn't use corporal punishment. He preferred verbal persuasion and, in extreme cases, the dunce cap. As he later wrote in the *Brooklyn Evening Star*:

To teach a good school it is not at all necessary for a man to be inflexible in rules and severe in discipline. Order and obedience we would always have; and yet two of the best schools we ever knew appeared always to the casual spectator to be complete uproar, confusion and chaos.

The District School that Whitman had attended, beginning at age five, used the Lancastrian Method of instruction—rote, question-and-answer drills—as if the factory methods of the Industrial Revolution could be transferred to education. It is unlikely that the young Whitman found anything enjoyable in it, and equally unlikely that he himself used it mechanistically when he taught. His newspaper editorials and articles glow with his love of children, so it is reasonable to assume that his manner was friendly toward his students.

In fact, Whitman probably had what we now call a humanistic approach to education. His ideas, as expressed in his newspaper articles and editorials, included close parent-teacher cooperation; teaching children to think for themselves and to moderate their own behavior; the teacher as friend and mentor instead of rigid authority figure; and the importance of understanding the subject as opposed to memorizing facts about it. Whitman felt that all children have potential and an appetite for knowledge, and that they should study "life," not just "books." He also thought that children should be taught music and have large playgrounds. He praised one new school because it was well ventilated and the students' seats had backs.

Much of our information on Whitman and his ideas about education comes from his newspaper articles and editorials in the *Brooklyn Evening Star* (September 1845–March 1846) and the *Brooklyn Daily Eagle* (March 1846–January 1848), collected by Florence Bernstein Freedman in her interesting book *Walt Whitman Looks at the Schools*. Bernstein points out that of Whitman's thirty-three articles for the *Evening Star*, a third of them are about education. Before Whitman started working for the *Daily Eagle*, that paper had never carried an article on education; Whitman wrote a slew of them. This is even more impressive in light of the *Daily Eagle*'s format: four pages per issue, at least two and usually three of which were filled with advertisements and legal notices (see figure 2).

Although some of Whitman's articles are hack journalism, his education pieces give the reader a good sense of what he felt was important. Some of them, such as "The Country School House," are touching; others, such as the one in which he (the supreme extoller of loafing) *denounced* loafing among young men, are, in retrospect, surprising and unintentionally funny. (He also tells young men, "Swear not! smoke not! and rough-and-tumble not!")

Whitman's classroom included poetry; some people suspect that the poems he had his students memorize were his own. There are instructional passages in his poetry, too. Advising both poets and teachers in "By Blue Ontario's Shore," he wrote:

Are you he who would assume a place to teach or be a poet here in the States?
The place is august, the terms obdurate.

Who would assume to teach here may well prepare himself body and mind,

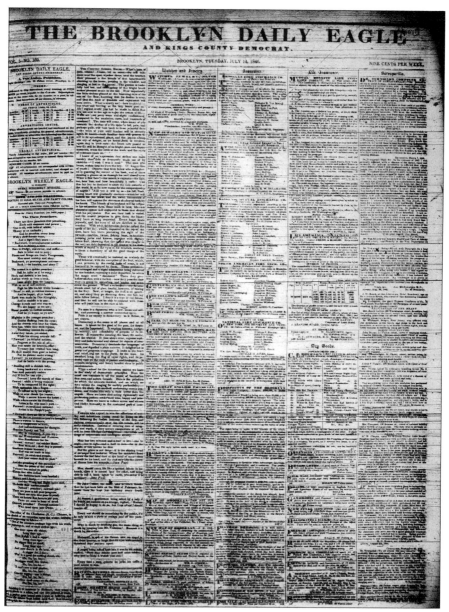

Fig. 2: Front page of the Brooklyn Daily Eagle, *July 14, 1846, with Whitman's article, "The Country School House," upper left.*

He may well survey, ponder, arm, fortify, harden, make lithe himself,
He shall surely be question'd beforehand by me with many and stern
    questions.
Who are you indeed who would talk or sing to America?
Have you studied out the land, its idioms and men?
Have you learn'd the physiology, phrenology, politics, geography, pride,
    freedom, friendship of the land? its substratums and objects?
Have you consider'd the organic compact of the first day of the first year
    of Independence, sign'd by the Commissioners, ratified by the States,
    and read by Washington at the head of the army?
Have you possess'd yourself of the Federal Constitution?
Do you see who have left all feudal processes and poems behind them,
    and assumed the poems and processes of Democracy?
Are you faithful to things? do you teach what the land and sea, the
    bodies of men, womanhood, amativeness, heroic angers, teach?
Have you sped through fleeting customs, popularities?
Can you hold your hand against all seductions, follies, whirls, fierce
    contentions? are you very strong? are you really of the whole People?
Are you not of some coterie? some school or mere religion?
Are you done with reviews and criticisms of life? animating now to life
    itself?
Have you vivified yourself from the maternity of these States?
Have you too the old ever-fresh forbearance and impartiality?
Do you hold the like love for those hardening to maturity? for the last-
    born? little and big? and for the errant?
What is this you bring my America?

That's a pretty tough questionnaire, but Whitman himself was
as tough as he was tender. Pablo Neruda put it this way: "But
what really counts is that Walt Whitman was not afraid to
teach—which means to learn at the hands of life and undertake
the responsibility of passing on the lesson!"

Notes: Much of the information in this piece comes from Florence
Bernstein Freedman's *Walt Whitman Looks at the Schools* (New York:
King's Crown Press, Columbia University, 1950). Unfortunately the
book is out of print and not easy to find.
   The Neruda quotation is from his "We Live in a Whitmanesque Age,"
a speech delivered to P.E.N. in 1972. It is included in *Walt Whitman:
The Measure of His Song* (Minneapolis: Holy Cow! Press, 1981), eds. Jim
Perlman, Ed Folsom, and Dan Campion.

Whitman on Education
Three Articles from the *Brooklyn Daily Eagle*

THE COUNTRY SCHOOL HOUSE. What a hum of little voices! Come, let us enter—we will take seats near the open window there, next the teacher. How pleasant is the breath of that honeysuckle climbing up the house, peeping in the window, and clinging at last to the eaves. The garden is tastefully laid out, and the rippling of the bright brook makes pleasant music to the ear. How impatiently the little urchins glance to the lessening rays of the sun on the floor, knowing that his decline is near, and that the hour of freedom and enjoyment will soon arrive. What a sturdy set!—how healthful!—but what sad fretting as the lazy hours pass on! Ah! rogues, could you but be made to think that you are now at the age to enjoy the cream of life—What are your petty woes and slight confinement, compared to the anxieties, cares and trammels of manhood? The time will come, when many of you towards the decline of a life spent in toil, pain, and perhaps guilt, will look back to those peaceful days—the voice of your mild teacher will in memory again be heard—each familiar face will present itself in its accustomed place, and the joyous whoop and cry of delight, as ye bound forth to freedom, again ring in your ears—the hours now passed so heavily will be thought of as bright, pure and happy moments, when the strife of the world and the cares of existence, come on.

I know of no expression that strikes one more forcibly than that so frequently made use of by children—"I wish I was a man." The man who hears, wishes that he were the boy. O! happy time of youth! Observe that little fellow who is employed in gnawing the corner of his book, and at times stealing a glance at us through his half closed eyes. What a fine face!—his mouth is exquisite—his hair, too, how fine, and how beautifully it curls! Can this fair boy be destined to abide the rude assaults of the world, fit as he now seems for the companionship of angels? And yet it will be so—his full, fresh, young heart will gradually contract—wrinkles will deform his fair brow, and the sweet lineaments of his face will assume the sternness shadowed forth by his heart. The friends of his boyhood will far eclipse in his estimation then, those made in later life—his pleasures appear dull compared to those now shared with his playmates. But see, their task is ended, and the master prepares to give them the liberty they have so long coveted. Every heart beats joyously, and the eyes of all are directed to their teacher. With what deliberation does he collect the spoils of the day, which, deposited on the top of the desk, have lain there provoking the sight of the owners—marbles, twine, fishing lines, te-to-tums, jumping jacks and knives, together with slightly bitten fruit, (showing that the culprit was caught in the act) are duly deposited in the drawer of his desk, which is sacred in the eyes of his scholars, seeming to them a depository of all the good things of the earth.

These will eventually be restored, as rewards for good behavior, with the exception of the fruit, which, I can perceive by the rueful looks of some, is not destined to be enjoyed by them. These preliminaries arranged and a slight admonition being delivered by the teacher, enjoining a quiet departure, he utters the magic word "dismissed." There they go—helter-skelter, with a racket—now they pass the door way—a group lie sprawling, and apples and pears strew the ground. What a scramble!—My favorite stands aloof, full of glee, fearful, however, of mixing in the fray. Now, at length, the fruit is all pouched, and away they go shouting down the hill, my little fellow behind. I fear it is a type of the future, and that he will not be able to contend with those who will jostle him in the race of life.

(July 14, 1846)

•

EDUCATION—SCHOOLS, ETC. In our prevalent system of Common School Instruction, there is far too much of mere forms and words. Boys and girls learn "lessons" in books, pat enough to the tongue, but vacant to the brain. Many wearisome hours are passed in getting this rote, which is almost useless, while the proper parts of education have been left unattended to. Of what use is it, for instance, that a boy knows the technical definition of a promontory or a gulf—and can bound states, as they are bounded in the book, north, and east, and south, and west, when he has no practical idea of the situation and direction of countries, and of the earth's different parts? Of what use is it that he can recite the rules of grammar, and speak off all its book terms, when he does not apply it in his conversation, knows not a tittle of the meaning of what he says, and is hourly committing the grossest violations of it? Of what use is it to a child that he has "ciphered through the book," to use the common phrase, when he cannot apply the various rules to the transactions of business, and is puzzled by a little simple sum perhaps in the very elementary parts of arithmetic?

Unless what is taught in a school be understood, and has some greater value than merely a knowledge of the words which convey it, it is all a sham. In schools (as too much in religion) many people have been too long accustomed to look at the *mere* form—the outward circumstance—without attending to the reality. It matters little that a teacher preserves the most admirable discipline—performs all the time-honored floggings and thumpings and cuffings—and goes through with all the old-established ceremonies of schoolteaching—unless the pupils are aided in forming sharp, intelligent minds—and are properly advanced in the branches they may be pursuing. Without these follow, his education is a mockery—a make believe. The forms of a school are of small account, except as they contribute to the main object—improvement.

The proper education of a child comprehends a great deal more than is generally thought of. Sending him to school, and learning him to read and write, is not educating him. That brings into play but a small part of his powers. A proper education unfolds and develops every faculty in its just proportions. It commences at the beginning, and leads him along the path step by step. Its aim is not to give so much book-learning, but to polish and invigorate the mind—to make it used to thinking and acting for itself, and to imbue it with a love for knowledge. It seeks to move the youthful intellect to reason, reflect and judge, and exercise its curiosity and powers of thought. True, these powers, this reason and judgment have to be exercised at first on childish subjects—but every step carries him further and further. What was even at first not difficult, becomes invaluable as an easy habit. And it is astonishing how much may be done in this way; how soon a child acquires, by proper training, a quickness of perception and a ready facility of drawing on stores of its own, that put to the blush the faculties of many, even of mature age. We consider it a great thing in education that the learner be taught to rely upon himself. The best teachers do not profess to *form* the mind, but to *direct* it in such a manner—and put such tools in its power—that it builds up itself. This part of education is far more worthy of attention, than the acquiring of a certain quantity of school knowledge. We would far rather have a child possessed of a bright, intelligent, moderately disciplined mind, joined to an inquisitive disposition, with very little of what is called learning, than to have him versed in all the accomplishments of the most forward of his age, arithmetic, grammar, Greek, Latin, and French, without that brightness and intelligence.

(November 23, 1846)

•

AN HOUR IN ONE OF THE BROOKLYN PUBLIC SCHOOLS. SOMETHING MORE ABOUT EDUCATION AND TEACHERS. We spent the greater part of Tuesday morning (2nd) in Public School No. 4, Classon Ave. near Flushing Ave. The building is not like our down-town school-houses: it is not near as convenient and durable, being built of wood, and somewhat shabby at that. We would take advantage of the occasion to suggest to the school officers of the 4th district and to the Board of Education, the fine opportunity they have of purchasing cheaply *now* in East Brooklyn two or three ample sites for school-houses, for the future.

Any body can see that in a very few years that thriving section of our city is to be to the rest somewhat as the valley of the Mississippi is to the other part of the Union. Children already abound there, and it is quite shocking that the places of their education should be cramped into a small compass, with mean play-grounds, and stifled closeness. And those evils can be so easily precluded. Fifteen hundred dollars will buy six lots in many of those streets; and such a surface would afford quite a handsome site for a seminary which would, in a few years, be filled with the people's children to overflowing. . . . The little people of No. 4 were all busily at work—some at one thing, some at another. We were quite pleased at the absence of the frozenness of restraint—that irksome and unnecessary discipline—which pervades some schools. They were at work studying and reciting industriously, but (as young people best perform those offices) like creatures of volition, and not like iron machinery. We saw many very fair specimens of writing—some good pencil sketches, in the way of drawing—and listened to exercises in grammar, arithmetic, and geography. In the first branch, we are free to say, we never saw the pupils in any public school who seemed so thoroughly to understand the *principles* of that study. They delved out the hidden grammatical position of words, that might have puzzled wiser heads—analyzed the parts of sentences, and, by comparison, soon got at the right of some pretty close questions. In arithmetic, too, the boys, (our time did not permit us to pay more than a passing look in the girls' school, and the primary,) showed that *things* were among them of more importance than mere *signs*—that the artificial of learning did not there carry the day, over the real. Among many bright boys, (they were *all* bright, and it's hardly fair perhaps to select out only a few, after all,) were Wm. Husted, T. H. Taylor, and two brothers named Van Voorhis. The classes ran over some other of their studies—and, upon the whole, made a marked impression of a favorable kind on us. We think this school an unanswerable argument in favor of treating youth at school as rational creatures—treating them gently, and instructing them in such a way that they *understand*, and *not* merely get by rote.—The whipping system should be entirely abolished in every school; and it is a scandal on the judgment and efficiency of any teacher who practices it, and any school officer who allows it. The absurd old way of teachers holding themselves aloof from their pupils, and punishing them for errors of mere manner, is exploded; and the day has come when instructors of the ancient kind must either yield to the better light, or fade before it. . . . In accordance with our custom, in narrating visits to our Brooklyn schools, we shall improve the chance to jot down a few hints on the matter of education and teachers—which matter really involves the weightiest issues to every man, woman, and child, everywhere. For what can be of higher consequence to a human being than his own mind, his temper, and his knowledge? The mere ordinary objects of wealth, politics, and so on, are comparatively insignificant to them.

Education, then, is a great subject. Its necessity and value require to be raised in the estimation of men. It is enough spoken about, but it needs to be more felt and acted upon. Mighty things depend upon the young of the age. Each little child has an immortal soul. He has the treasure house of the human mind; and it depends upon those who ought to see to his education, whether the costly and precious beauties of that treasure house shall be locked up for ever; or brought forth to gladden the eyes of men, and prove a perpetual spring of delight to their now unconscious possessor. Fully to bring out these boundless capacities requires hard and laborious attention. Nothing will do but the sleepless eye and the ever guarding hand. Why what mighty energies lie slumbering at this moment in the brains of the school-children of Brooklyn!—destined in many of them to slumber for ever, for the want of being brought forth to the day! energies, equal without doubt, to the performance of great deeds—to the gaining of deathless fame and glory; or what is better still of benefiting the condition of mankind. What wondrous things might be done were a complete education, in the comprehensive sense of the term, given to those children. Possibly at some future time, the balance of a nation's happiness might be made to rise or fall by one of their hands. Who can look down into the dark vista of the future, and say what bright path shall not be marked out for some of them? Like as arrows in the hands of the giant, says the Bible, even so are young children: happy is he who hath his quiver full of them.

The first requirement for those who have charge of the young, appears to be that their physical well-being, their health and comfort be attended to. The next undoubtedly is with regard to their moral nature. This is an all-important part. In youth are laid the foundations of the character far deeper and far more firmly than we generally imagine. That is the time to make them good and honest, and lovers of truth. The mind is then a new ground—virgin soil. Whatever seeds are dropt there, they will take root and grow up as the child grows up, and bear either the bitter and poisonous or the sweet and grateful fruit. And the virtues should be planted then deeply and carefully. Honesty and strict adherence to truth, those mighty anchors of true religion, in that early season of life should be carefully inwoven with the very fibres of the heart. No anxiety can be too great, and no labor too severe, or care too incessant, if they can but effect this purpose. Day and night it should be the great aim. Every occasion should be seized, and every interruption jealously watched, that can influence this important matter. To plant in the heart of a child this purity, this love of truth, and this beautiful innocence from all evil intentions, ought to be a parent's fondest wish and strongest effort. And when the harvest comes, how richly will he be repaid. To know that honest and upright dispositions are as natural to his child as are the beatings of his heart, will repay him back a thousand fold for all his toil and all his anxiety. And let no one suppose that it is so difficult a task to make the mind of a child moral and virtuous. It is this wicked world—it is the corruption which accumulates in the habits and thoughts of society—that make the young, as they grow up become more and more deficient in virtue. But it is no impossible task, with proper management, to make a sincere and truth-loving child. Their brains will receive and nourish good propensities as well, if not easier than bad ones. . . . He or she is a foolish parent who thinks that care and labor for a child can be spent in any more desirable way than in making it the possessor of a heart wherein dwell integrity and pure thoughts, and hatred of all kinds of falsehood, and meanness and dishonesty. Desirable as we consider learning to be, we consider an honest soul to be far, far more desirable. Learning is the key which unlocks to us the minds of the wise, and the beauties of creation, and the lofty pleasures of intellect. But a pure soul is the key that unlocks the very gates of paradise: and therefore it is the very perfection of wisdom to confer on the young that which is most precious. And there is this difference: that while the branches of learning are easiest of access to the children of the opulent, who can best afford the time and expense, the indigent man can train up *his* children to have honest minds and character, as cheaply and as easily as the richest in the land. And the poorest man on earth, with an upright heart, and unblemished reputation, stands forth, yes towers up like a pillar of beauty, by the side of the richest and proudest, whose minds conscious of wrongs done, and consciences seared, and bad desires given way to, shrink to littleness before his.

It is very common to hear people say that education is a great thing. We question though whether one in a hundred of those who talk this way ever act out the undoubted truism which is in their mouths. Very few persons are so stupid as not to acknowledge that it is desirable to have learning. —But are such men willing to take proper pains and trouble to procure this important requisite for their children, or those under their charge? Do they find out about the teacher who is to superintend their children's education? Do they visit the school? Do they carefully examine from time to time whether a reasonable progress is made? It is true, to do so would be troublesome: it might cost them a few hours every month, and would require some little exercise of the judgment; and so it is generally left undone. Now if it were a question where the loss or gain of dollars was concerned, would these same individuals be thus inattentive? But, says some one, I pay for my children's schooling and I send them to school; is not that enough? No: it is not enough. In such an important matter as the education of the young, each parent should see for himself, and not trust to chance. He should have frequent conferences with the teacher, arranging what studies ought to be pursued, and the management of the children, and the procuring of proper books and other appliances for learning. It should be his business to see that the person who conducts the school is a competent person, having in himself no deficiencies or characteristics that unfit him for the station. He should also be careful that every reasonable facility be given to forward his children in their studies, and to increase their confidence and respect for their teacher. . . . We do not hesitate to say, too, that it depends as much upon the parent at home, as upon the teacher at school, whether the child learns even at school. The parent and teacher should work together with the same object at heart. It is a sure death-blow to a teacher's influence over any child, when that child is taught at home to find fault with or think contemptuously of his teacher. —For the great lever in education at school is the confidence of a child in his master. This is a mighty power. With it an intelligent teacher can do wonders. But when a parent is unwise enough to let his child be impressed with the idea that his master is blamable and wrong, that he is a person set up for the purpose of wearing out whips upon boys' backs, or is a tyrant, and does not deserve to be respected by his pupils, then the charm is broken; then the best influence of the teacher over the child, the influence of love, is gone; and for all the good he gets, the youthful learner may as well be kept at home.

A great deal depends too upon making a school pleasant. Any teacher who loses sight of this, commits a great error. Who has not heard that such or such a one has learned some particular accomplishment or trade with very remarkable quickness and perfection, because he "took a fancy to it," and was pleased with it? Has it never entered into the thoughts of those who send to school that it is possible for their children to take a fancy for, and be pleased with, their school, and to improve in their studies there with much more rapidity in consequence? It is evidently then a great object gained when the school is loved and sought, not hated and shunned; and those persons make a capital mistake, if they would but be aware of it, who let their young people be sent to the school room, impressed with the idea that it is a prison, or a dreary and tiresome place. With regard to this last point, we are clear of the good of singing exercises in schools. A more innocent amusement, and one practised with better results, both as regards its beneficial aid to other studies and its giving a gentle tone to the passions and tempers of children, there is not.

(March 4, 1847)

My High School English Teacher

by Allen Ginsberg

During my junior and senior years in high school in Paterson, New Jersey, the outstanding, classic, Sherwood Andersonesque character was a Miss Frances Durban, who was a lady weighing perhaps 250 or 300 pounds, of immense girth and humor, who dressed in blue dresses with lace around the neck. She taught Walt Whitman by reading him aloud with tremendous enthusiasm, in particular the lines, "I find no fat sweeter than that which sticks to my own bones . . ." (and I have to paraphrase the rest: "the odor wafting from my body . . . admire my own armpits . . . breasts . . . feet . . .").

I still remember Frances Durban's smell wafting across the classroom on hot May days. There was an awful body odor from such a sweating mass of fat. Somehow, repulsive as that was, her cherubic round face, half-smile, and huge-girthed laughter were miracles of pleasure and energy that imprinted Whitman on my head forever. Her presentation of his humor and self-acceptance was decisive in turning me on, not merely to his sympathy, not merely to his empathies, not merely to his range, but also to his humorous intelligence.

I had home teachings of all poetry, including Whitman, particularly, from my father. Whitman was on the curriculum in high school, too, so I knew something about his work, particularly "When Lilacs Last in the Dooryard Bloom'd." But Frances Durban specialized in the self-acceptance poems in "Song of Myself."

The Ceaseless Rings
of Walt Whitman

by Langston Hughes

Walt Whitman, greatest of American poets, was born on a farm owned by his father near West Hills, Long Island, New York, on the last day of May, 1819. He died in a tiny old house of his own on Mickle Street in Camden, New Jersey, at the end of March, 1892. The span of his life ran from American slavery through the Civil War to American freedom and the approaching dawn of the twentieth century.

Whitman did not fight in the War Between the States. He hated war and killing, but he devoted much of his time to nursing and caring for the wounded, both Northern and Southern, white or Negro, Yankee or Rebel. At Culpeper, Virginia, a staging area, he saw enough of combat to sicken him against war. But on errands of mercy, he went out to the battlefields and into field hospitals. From his friends he solicited money to buy cookies, candies, ice cream, magazines, and papers for the wounded. He tended them, read to them, wrote letters home for those who could not write, and cheered them with stories. He helped those with leg injuries to learn to walk again.

In 1864, assisting a surgeon in an amputation, Walt Whitman was accidentally cut with a gangrenous scalpel. An infection set in which caused him health complications in later life. While carrying on this voluntary nursing among the wounded in and near Washington, Whitman held a job as a clerk in the Indian Office. The attacks of narrow-minded readers on his poetry caused him to lose this job. But, through the help of friends, he secured a place in the Attorney General's office. In the late night hours, he continued to write his poems of democracy, articles, and letters for the papers.

His position in the Indian Office was not the first that Whitman had lost because of his liberal views. He had been an editor of the *Brooklyn Eagle*, but was fired there in 1848 because he refused to support Governor Cass of Michigan who advocated the continuation of slavery. Whitman called people like Cass "Dough Faces," because of their condonance of Southern slavery.

Whitman abhorred slave catchers and those who gave them aid or supported their political beliefs. In the *New York Evening Post*, Whitman wrote:

We are all docile dough-faces,
They knead us with the fist,
They, the dashing Southern Lords,
We labor as they list.
For them we speak—or hold our tongue,
For them we turn and twist.

There had been a half-dozen or so slaves on the ancestral Whitman farm, and young Walt had played with them as a child. Perhaps that is where he acquired his sympathy for the Negro People, and his early belief that all men should be free—a belief that grew to embrace the peoples of the whole world, expressed over and over throughout his poems, encompassing not only America but the colonial peoples, the serfs of tsarist Russia, the suppressed classes everywhere. His spiritual self roamed the earth wherever the winds of freedom blow however faintly, keeping company with the foiled revolutionaries of Europe or the suppressed coolies of Asia.

Because the vast sweep of democracy is still incomplete even in America today, because revolutionaries seeking to break old fetters are still foiled in Europe and Asia, because the physical life of the Brooklyn ferries and the Broadway street cars and the Mississippi river banks and the still fresh battlefields of World War II continue to pulse with the same heartbeats of humanity as in Whitman's time, his poetry strikes us now with the same immediacy it must have awakened in its earliest readers in the 1850s.

The good gray poet of democracy is one of literature's great faithholders in human freedom. Speaking simply for people everywhere and most of all for the believers in our basic American dream, he is constantly growing in stature as the twentieth century advances and edition after edition of his poems appears.

Walt Whitman wrote without the frills, furbelows, and decorations of conventional poetry, usually without rhyme or measured prettiness. Perhaps because of his simplicity, timid poetry lovers over the years have been frightened away from his *Leaves of Grass*, poems as firmly rooted and as brightly growing as the grass itself. Perhaps, too, because his all-embracing words lock arms with workers and farmers, Negroes and whites, Asiatics and Europeans, serfs and free men, beaming democracy to all, many academic-minded intellectual isolationists in America have had little use for Whitman, and so have impeded his handclasp with today by keeping him imprisoned in silence on library shelves. Still his words leap from their pages and their spirit grows steadily stronger everywhere.

The best indication of the scope of Whitman's poems might be found in his own "Song of the Answerer" where he writes about poetry:

. . . I give the sign of democracy.
By God! I will accept nothing which all cannot have their counterpart of on the same terms . . .

So there is no keeping Whitman imprisoned in silence. He proclaims:

I ordain myself loosed of limits. . . .
Going where I list. . . .
Gently, but with undeniable will, divesting myself of the holds that would hold me.

One of the greatest "I" poets of all time, Whitman's "I" is not the "I" of the introspective versifiers who write always and only about themselves. Rather it is the cosmic "I" of all peoples who seek freedom, decency, and dignity, friendship and equality between individuals and races all over the world.

The words of true poems give you more than poems,
They give you to form for yourself poems, religions, politics, war, peace, behavior, histories, essays, daily life and everything else,
They balance ranks, colors, races, creeds, and the sexes . . .
They bring none to his or her terminus or to be content and full,
Whom they take they take into space to behold the birth of stars, to learn one of the meanings,
To launch off with absolute faith, to sweep through the ceaseless rings and never be quiet again.

In this atomic age of ours, when the ceaseless rings are multiplied a million fold, the Whitman spiral is upward and outward toward a freer, better life for all, not narrowing downward toward death and destruction. Singing the greatness of the individual, Whitman also sings the greatness of unity, cooperation, and understanding:

> . . . all the men ever born are also my brothers, and the women my sisters. . . .

As an after-thought he adds:

> (I am large, I contain multitudes).

Certainly, his poems contain us all. The reader cannot help but see his own better self therein.

Whitman's Informal History of His Times: *Democratic Vistas* & *Specimen Days*

by Gary Lenhart

After the Civil War, Walt Whitman continued to revise and expand *Leaves of Grass*. He also produced two major prose works: *Democratic Vistas* and *Specimen Days*. *Democratic Vistas* was written between the end of the Civil War and 1871, while he was employed as a clerk in the Attorney General's office in Washington. Though it was composed over a number of years, Whitman organized it into a coherent, if not seamless, essay about the future of the United States. The changes that the Civil War wrought in the country that Whitman had celebrated in *Leaves of Grass* were already becoming clear, and it was the appropriate time to contemplate the paths that the country had taken and the choices that were still to be made. The years immediately following the Civil War are notorious for graft, profiteering, carpetbagging, and the rise of a new class of the superrich commonly referred to as "robber barons." The Civil War also marked the transformation of the United States from a country of small landholders to a nation of industrial workers. Whitman was quick to see that industrialization posed new dangers to American democracy and was perceptive enough to note the inglorious strands in the nation's fabric that were apparent long before the war.

Democratic Vistas is both a justification for and corrective to *Leaves of Grass*. Whitman now calls for America to recognize qualities in the native character that he had celebrated in *Leaves of Grass* as already burgeoning. For the poet, the heroism of the common soldier, and particularly the wounded or dying soldier, in the Civil War was in many ways a confirmation of the tribute he had already paid to the American people. But as he saw businessmen and politicians seizing on the war's deprivations and dislocations to extort outrageous profits, his enthusiasm for the special nobility of a democratic people was tempered.

Specimen Days avoids this difficult period entirely. It begins with Whitman's family history and his own prewar experience, continues with wartime notes about his service to the wounded in Washington hospitals, skips the next ten years to his convalescence in Camden, New Jersey, and along rural Timber Creek (not far from Camden) following the stroke that removed him from Washington, and includes his once-again buoyant reflections on the nation as he travels about it as the renowned "good gray poet." A collection of writings that spans more than thirty years, *Specimen Days* consists of "diary-jottings," "war memoranda," "nature notes," travel observations, and "odds and ends" from the last ten years of his life, including excerpts from letters to friends. He remarked that the book is "probably without any definite purpose that can be told in a statement" and called it "the most wayward, spontaneous, fragmentary book ever printed." To retain their freshness and flavor, these fragments are fastened together with a minimum of cement and are full of "skips and jumps." Most of *Specimen Days* was written during periods when Whitman was unemployed or retired, and it has a leisurely and reflective character.

Together, these two works constitute a marvelous informal history of nineteenth-century America, from Whitman's earliest memories, which date back to the late 1820s, to the publication of *Specimen Days* in 1882.

"Convulsiveness": New Form for New Literature

In *Specimen Days*, Whitman admits that he has occasionally feared that his notes would prove "but a batch of convulsively written reminiscences."[*] But he does not apologize for this. Instead he claims that such convulsiveness best reflects the war that is his subject. His notes "are but parts of the actual distraction, heat, smoke, and excitement" of the war (p. 480). So the "form" of his book finds the character of his subject. This attitude toward art, that it should retain an air of spontaneity and reflect the circumstances of composition, is still considered experimental.

---

[*]Mark Van Doren, ed., *The Portable Walt Whitman* (New York: Penguin, 1977), p. 480. All the references in this essay are to that edition.

I believe that Whitman conceived his prose as "democratic" in form, i.e., avoiding any hierarchy of importance or architectural ordering. He is open to whatever catches his attention at the moment. The bees count as much as Thomas Carlyle, the birds as much as President Hayes. Though *Specimen Days* is diaristic, there is nothing daily about it. Instead, it is a series of epiphanies, but epiphanies of the common, the average, the random. In *Specimen Days*, Whitman implies that every moment is worthwhile, if only we can properly attend to it. Of course we don't, because we are frequently distracted. But the emphasis has shifted from the drama of the moment to the quality of attention that the artist brings to the moment. Such a conception of art goes hand in hand with democratic political impulses. Just as we now consider all humans to be born equal, so must all kinds of lives and all types of environments be worthy of our attention. Long before Freud, artists were bringing into consciousness that part of the story of the world that had previously been considered unworthy of memory or celebration. Some people lament that artists no longer treat "grand" subjects. In Whitman's case, it wasn't that he didn't treat the grand subjects, but that he set them alongside the low and the ordinary. He does address the greatest political event of his time, the Civil War, and great personages of his time, Lincoln, Grant, Emerson, Carlyle. But he does not "build" to those passages, or present them as the greatest part of his tale. He recognizes that many of his era's heroes are unknown and destined to remain so: "No formal general's report, nor book in the library, nor column in the paper, embalms the bravest, north or south, east or west. Unnamed, unknown, remain, and still remain, the bravest soldiers" (pp. 424–425). Later he again notes that "the real war," the story of the actual soldier, "will never be written" (p. 483).

When he describes the president, he emphasizes Lincoln's unassuming aspect. In those pre-air-conditioning days, the President and his family slept out of town during the hot season. The path from the Lincolns' summer residence to the White House passed by Whitman's lodgings, so Whitman had occasion daily to view the man. He says the President "looks about as ordinary in attire, etc., as the commonest man" (p. 434). When the President travels in his barouche with Mrs. Lincoln, Whitman points out that "the equipage is of the plainest kind, only two horses, and they nothing extra" (p. 435). Of course, Lincoln also stressed the common part of his humanity, that he was born in a log cabin and was a simple country lawyer. It remains part of the mythology of the United States that everyone is self-made from such humble origins. (Even those who grow up among America's richest families, people like Alfred Bloomingdale and Donald Trump, really seem to believe that they are "self-made men.") Both Lincoln and Whitman dressed the part: Lincoln most often in a plain black suit, and Whitman with his shirt open at the collar, like a common laborer.

Long Island and Family Background

Although Whitman begins *Specimen Days* with a history of his family and a description of the Long Island of his boyhood, this section of the book was written later than most of the rest. The Long Island that Walt Whitman describes is almost unrecognizable to a modern reader. In his advanced age, he recalled Long Island as rustic and idyllic, a generous and underpopulated stretch of farmland and beach that seemed even more extensive to a boy. But it's interesting to note too that already by 1820 his family had migrated a great deal. In the history of the two branches of his family, from the seventeenth to the nineteenth centuries, one can read a tale of restless individual comings and goings, of national and regional booms and busts.

The pattern of westward migration is so well established in our national consciousness that we forget that the migrations have gone both ways. We think of American families as arriving on the East Coast, setting out for the West, and settling down to build a farm, with generations descending therefrom. But the pattern is much more one of endless movement and flux, of pulling up stakes and heading back East as much as setting out for the West, of sons and daughters gone off to distant parts, and the return of those who strike it rich to the Eastern Seaboard or even to Europe. One notes too how quickly the Whitman family moves from a spartan farming existence to become tradesmen and speculators (in his father's case, a carpenter and small real estate developer in Brooklyn).

People and Institutions

Though Whitman is the advocate of scientific progress and a new democratic civilization, he is wary of some modern forms of social organization, particularly those that contribute to specialization. He hankers for a literature that addresses itself not to a particular "coterie," but to every individual. While he stresses the importance of history, he is dissatisfied with history that is for "technists" (p. 352). He stresses the "religious element" as perhaps the most important for a nation but does not find it in churches. He urges young men (this is before the 19th Amendment to the Constitution gave women the suffrage) to vote and become involved in politics, but he despises politicians.

Whitman is famed for his celebration of the American people and his faith in democracy. He devoted his life to a literature "of the people, by the people, and for the people," even though the popular response to his work was less enthusiastic than he had hoped. He thought that the great literatures of feudal Europe, even the works of Shakespeare and Dante, had never recognized "the people" (by which he meant *all* the people, including the most humble), and thus continued to be justifications for the old monarchic orders.

Whitman was not an adherent of the Great Man theory of history. He didn't have much faith in America's leaders. ("Our leading men are not of much account and never have been" [p. 579]). In fact, his view of politicians was that "shams, etc., will always be the show, like ocean's scum; enough, if waters deep and clear make up the rest" (p. 342). Though he admires President Grant, he admits that the General is a "mere plain man—no art, no poetry" with "absolutely no pronounc'd genius or conventional eminence of any kind" (p. 580). It is in the very lack of anything heroic about Grant, his commonness, that Whitman finds cause to be optimistic about the future of the U.S. He revises his ideas of oratory after reading President Hayes's speeches "on easy topics not too deep" (p. 581). Though conceding that they are "wanting in dignity," he finds them "just what they should be, considering all the circumstances, who they come from, and who they are addressed to" (p. 581).

On occasion he also laments the character of the average American. He thinks the American people "the most peaceful and money making [and] the most restless and most warlike" people on earth. Five years after the war that confirmed his opinions of the great heroism of the average man, the common soldier, he already perceives that "never was there, perhaps, more hollowness of heart than at present, and here in the United States. . . . The spectacle is appalling. We live in an atmosphere of hypocrisy throughout" (p. 325). A revenue agent assures him that the business classes are even more depraved than supposed. In the government, every office is for sale.

But by the time of his Western jaunt, he has recovered his faith in the American people and even in American institutions, as demonstrated by his comments on Grant and Hayes.

The Civil War

In *A Backward Glance o'er Traveled Roads*, published in 1888, Whitman says of his experiences during the Civil War that "without those three or four years and the experiences they gave, *Leaves of Grass* would not now be existing" (p. 307). Since a hefty chunk of the book was published in 1855, six years before the war began, the old poet's words may not be a reliable judgment upon it. But they do reveal how central Whitman believed the war was to his life and work and how keenly he felt his experience during the war. And if there can be a difference of opinion about the importance of the war to Whitman's poems, there can be no such disagreement about its central place in *Specimen Days* and *Democratic Vistas*.

Whitman, who was in Brooklyn at the time of the war's outbreak, reports that sentiment there was similar to sentiment among editorial writers and politicians at the beginning of any war: let's get in there and kick them in the pants and then bring the boys home (p. 407). But it was soon clear that the war would not end quickly, nor without great expense and sacrifice.

Whitman went down to the battlefields to look for his brother and then spent the war working in the hospitals in and around Washington. Hospital duty provides a sobering view of any war, confronting one daily with the war's casualties and not its unscathed conquerors. But the Civil War's hospitals were made particularly gruesome by their extent (in sheer numbers, the Civil War was awesomely destructive) and by advances in military technology that put it years ahead of military tactics and medical treatment. There were an extraordinary number of amputations, many performed without anesthesia (but perhaps with enough whisky to get the patient drunk), and because the wounded lay on the battlefield for long periods before they could be retrieved, infection and gangrene were widespread. The Civil War is often said to be the first "modern" war; more soldiers were killed than in all other American wars combined. Much of the killing was done in hand-to-hand combat, but much of it was also impersonal and accidental (the result of artillery shelling of dugout positions), making it all the more terrible.

Whitman was from New York and unabashedly partial to the Union side of the conflict, but his sympathies extended to soldiers of the Confederacy. *Specimen Days* gives us an intimate and often surprising view of the Union army. It was comprised of more Southerners than one might think (there were more Union soldiers from the slave state Kentucky than Napoleon had in his entire army at Waterloo), of a substantial number of immigrants (about one in ten), of a disproportionately large number of farmboys from all over the states, and of many "colored" troops.

Whitman heard firsthand tales from former prisoners of war about the brutal conditions in Southern prisons, and firsthand accounts of war atrocities from soldiers who were witnesses and even participants in the slaughter. In one of the most hair-raisingly ferocious anecdotes in all the annals of war, he relates how one big rebel soldier was "mortally wounded top of the head, so that the brains partially exuded. He lived three days, lying on his back on the spot where he first dropt. He dug with his heel in the ground during that time a hole big enough to put in a couple of ordinary knapsacks. He just lay there in the open air, and with little intermission kept his heel going night and day" (p. 447).

Although he is not untouched by tales of battlefield glory, for him the greatest heroism is in the hospital. For instance, he describes a parade of cavalry as "the most inspiriting of all war shows" (p. 429), but he concludes his description of the parade by noting the string of ambulances that followed it, "bearing a large load of wounded" in another direction.

Whitman touches on the politics and grand personages of the war, but his memoirs are for the most part a history of common soldiers (he would say "the common soldier") bearing duress with fortitude and good humor. Whitman passes among them handing out writing paper, fresh fruit, toiletries, and small change. He spends hours sitting by their beds, reading to them or silently holding their hands, and, in some cases, helping them die. It is an ennobling picture of patient and nurse, surely among the most unsung heroes of any war.

"An Interregnum Paragraph"

This *Specimen Days* entry connects the two main "episodes" in the book, the Civil War jottings and the Timber Creek notes. After the war, Whitman remained in Washington until February 1873, when he suffered a stroke that resulted in partial paralysis and retired to Camden to recover. There he instituted his own regimen for recovery, traveling down to Timber Creek, a tributary of the Delaware River, where he bathed in the stream (scrubbing himself with a hard-bristled brush), wrestled with saplings, and reclined, oftimes nude, in the sun, reading, writing, and meditating. Despite his "invalidism," he claimed to get his share of fun, and said the "trick is, I find, to tone your wants and tastes low down enough, and make much of negatives, and of mere daylight and the skies" (p. 485).

Paragraphs from Timber Creek

The "nature-notes" that Whitman composed at Timber Creek are even more random than his memoirs of the war. A typical entry will note the colors of the woods in fall or the abundance of crows in late November, or will list the trees he has noticed in the country or the birds he has seen, and in no more remarkable fashion than any bird-watcher's list. They form an alternative to the immersion in wartime drama, as a reminder that the world turns irrespective of political or literary affairs. In some ways, they are the most intimate of all Whitman's writings, even more intimate than his poems. From Timber Creek, Whitman wishes to impart a new "lesson"—the restorative power of the open air: "Literature flies so high and is so hotly spiced, that our notes may seem hardly more than breaths of common air, or draughts of water to drink. But that is part of our lesson" (p. 485). (Wordsworth also claimed that the aim of poetry is to lower the threshold of human excitement, so to inspire people with common and sane incidents, and thus diminish their taste for the morbid and the extravagant.)

The Literary Life

It is common among literary historians to emphasize Whitman's isolation from American literary life. Part of this misconception stems from his continual disparagement of the writers of his time: "a parcel of dandies and ennuyés, dapper little gentlemen from abroad, who flood us with their thin sentiment of parlors, parasols, piano songs, tinkling rhymes, the five-hundredth importation—or whimpering and crying about something, chasing one aborted conceit after another, and forever occupied in dyspeptic amours with dyspeptic women" (363), or "Where is the man of letters, where is the book, with any nobler aim than to follow in the old track, repeat what has been said before—and, as its utmost triumph, sell well, and be erudite or elegant?" (363). But it is obvious to a reader of *Specimen Days* that Whitman was much more closely connected to American literary life than is generally thought. He is on speaking terms with William Cullen Bryant, Emerson, and Thoreau, and mentions his "friend, Joaquin Miller." His closest literary friend is perhaps John Burroughs, whom he visits several times at his home in the Catskills. He met Poe and saw James Fenimore Cooper, attended William Cullen Bryant's funeral. He includes in *Specimen Days* a "Tribute to Four Poets" — Emerson, Bryant, Longfellow, and Whittier. He gave the memorial oration at Lincoln Hall in Philadelphia on the 140th birthday of Thomas Paine. He frequented the opera (*Lucia di Lammermoor, I Puritani, Il Trovatore, The Barber of Seville*, and others) at which he must have met—or at least nodded to—other writers. He wrote as incisively about Carlyle as any of his contemporaries ("behind the tally of genius and morals stands the stomach, and gives a sort of casting vote") (p. 599), and managed a frank, complimentary eulogy for Longfellow.

The Western Jaunt

Nowhere is the pace of change in the American landscape more evident than in these pages recording Whitman's jaunt through the American West in 1879. The trains travel "like lightning through the night" and "danger adds zest" (p. 561). In fact, collisions were frequent; Whitman is delayed by one. The period during and just following the Civil War was perhaps the heyday of railroad building in America, much as the years following the Second World War saw air travel become the burgeoning mode of transport, at least for those who could afford it.

Whitman tells a story about life in the "early days" on the prairie that involves gunfighting and lynching. But this incident of the "early days" occurred in 1868, only eleven years prior to the time Whitman is writing! And yet, how much has changed. The buffalo plains, inhabited largely by Native Americans, had already become the "Golden Belt," "famed for its wheat" (p. 564). That means in just ten years the natives had been routed, farms built, fields planted, and a reputation for wheat production gained.

Whitman talks much about the literature of the prairies, though he doesn't find any examples of it. It's as if he is trying to summon into existence the literature he thinks the prairies deserve. He does realize, however, that "materialistic prosperity, in all its varied forms, . . . intercommunication and freedom, are first to be attended to" (p. 579).

Sometimes even the most ardent admirers of Whitman are dismayed by his grandiloquent declamations of a literature that doesn't yet exist and of a people who are still coming into being. But there's always another side to Whitman, the side that pays such fierce attention to the instant that his writings remain stunningly vital 100 years later. One of my favorite entries from his Western jaunt is the entry about the coreopsis, a "hardy little yellow five-petal'd September and October wild-flower" (p. 572). Right in the middle of remarks on Yellowstone National Park and the poetry of the Great Plains, he inserts a paragraph about this little wildflower that he has seen "on the Hudson and over Long Island, and along the banks of the Delaware and through New Jersey, (as years ago up the Connecticut, and one fall by Lake Champlain)" (p. 572), and the "millions" that he now sees along the entire route of his Western trip. It is in passages like these that Whitman's delight in the world's various bounty becomes undeniably infectious.

Women

During his service in Civil War hospitals, it became evident to Whitman that "few or no young ladies, under the irresistible conventions of society, answer the practical requirements of nurses for soldiers" (p. 457). He thought that only those who were mothers, and thus made unashamedly familiar with the human anatomy both male and female, were capable of serving competently as nurses. In *Democratic Vistas*, he attacks these conventions and calls for the freeing of women from these restrictions, for the redeeming of women out of "silliness, millinery, and every kind of dyspeptic depletion" (p. 328). He notes in the Western jaunt section of *Specimen Days* that he is especially disappointed with the women of the prairie cities, whom he finds "'intellectual' and fashionable," but "generally doll-like" (p. 579).

He gives specific examples of the kind of independent women he has in mind as models for America's future. Of course, in the aftermath of the Civil War, because of the shortage of able-bodied men, American women did increasingly take on roles and occupations previously denied them. But Whitman fondly remembers women who took on such roles before the war, when it was even less common. In fact, his mother seems to have been one of them.

Whitman celebrates motherhood particularly, and some critics cite his paeans to motherhood to suggest that the role he sees for women is limited to their maternal function. But anyone who reads all of *Leaves of Grass* or his essays knows that he is far more open to the day when women's entrance into the "arenas of practical life, politics, the suffrage, etc.," will be put to "real experiment" (p. 356).

As he wrote in *Leaves of Grass,* "The Female equally with the Male I sing" (p. 252). He not only believed in the equality of women in the eyes of the law (it would be another fifty years before women gained the right to vote), he believed that women must live in the world on equal terms with men. The women he celebrates in *Leaves of Grass* are not typical of the "supreme ideals of feminine excellence" represented by standard Victorian heroines:

They know how to swim, row, ride, wrestle, shoot, run, strike,
 retreat, advance, resist, defend themselves,
They are ultimate in their own right—they are calm, clear, well-
 possessed of themselves. (p. 168)

The Poet *al Fresco*

At the conclusion of both *Specimen Days* and *Democratic Vistas*, Whitman stresses the importance of being outdoors. As much of *Specimen Days* testifies, he spent a good deal of his life in the woods or at the ocean, and believed that books read out of doors had a different character than books read in the library or office. So, if he found a book cumbersome to tote to the woods, he would tear pages from it and take them along in his pocket. He goes so far as to say that he sees no hope for the flourishing or even sustaining of democracy in America if its citizens are not "vitalized by regular contact with outdoor light and air and growths, farm scenes, animals, fields, trees, birds, sunwarmth and free skies" (p. 640). At the beginning of his Timber Creek notes, he had proclaimed "the bracing and buoyant equilibrium of concrete outdoor Nature, the only permanent reliance for sanity of book or human life" (p. 485).

This reverence for "Nature" has been an abiding part of the American character almost since the nation's inception, but particularly since it became evident about the time of the Civil War that the American wilderness was not infinite. Although the population has been largely urban and suburban for a long time now, most Americans continue to agree with Whitman about the importance of frequent contact with Nature. Environmental and conservation organizations continue to appeal to Americans from across the political spectrum. Most surveys report that an overwhelming majority of Americans are willing to sacrifice and even pay higher taxes to maintain our national parks and green retreats. Even the sales of Winnebagos and other motor homes for the annual summer campground pilgrimage show how deeply rooted these American habits and beliefs are.

But Whitman's concerns with Nature and invocation of the *literatus al fresco* have specific historical roots. One thinks of his contemporaries in France, the Impressionist painters, who also were trooping to the country to experience a direct contact with Nature. Also, as Whitman mentions at the end of *Democratic Vistas*, by the end of the Civil War "the labor question" is "beginning to open like a yawning gulf" (p. 378). In both France and the U.S., the Industrial Revolution that had long been in progress was, by 1865, on the verge of transforming the country's lower classes from a majority of farmers and peasants to a labor force of urban factory workers. Such a transformation has profound effects on the national character. As Thomas Jefferson wrote, "We shall [remain virtuous] as long as agriculture is our principal object, which will be the case, while there remains vacant lands in any part of America. When we get piled upon one another in large cities, as in Europe, we shall become corrupt as in Europe, and go to eating one another as they do there."

By Whitman's time, the day that Jefferson feared (and thought to be far in the future) had arrived. Witnessing this major transformation in society, Whitman responds by insisting on the connection to Nature as an important measure of art's efficacy. His prescription for American authors: "A strong-fibered joyousness and faith, and the sense of health *al fresco*, may well enter into the preparation of future noble American authorship. Part of the test of a great literatus shall be the absence in him of the idea of the covert, the lurid, the maleficent, the devil, the grim estimates inherited from the Puritans, hell, natural depravity, and the like. The great literatus will be known, among the rest, by his cheerful simplicity, his adherence to natural standards, his limitless faith in God, his reverence, and by the absence in him of doubt, ennui, burlesque, persiflage, or any strained and temporary fashion" (p. 370).

Thirteen Outstanding Entries in *Specimen Days*

Specimen Days consists of several distinct parts: Whitman's "stock," the Civil War, his "nature notes" from Timber Creek, the Western jaunt, the Canada trip, and his reflections on contemporary literary figures. But the charm of the book is in its random musings, memorable interruptions, and varied digressions. These add up to a quirky, informal portrait of Whitman's times. But they do not suffer much when excerpted, and the book may be read as it was written, in "skips and jumps." Here I've selected a few of my favorite parts as a Baedeker for the traveler who doesn't have much time to spend in Whitman country.

• "My First Reading—Lafayette": In writing of his childhood, Whitman includes a footnote from John Burroughs's biography of Whitman that tells how the Marquis de Lafayette, on a triumphal visit to Brooklyn in 1824, picked up and kissed the five-year-old Walt Whitman. Although I don't understand why Whitman quotes Burroughs, who could not have had the story from any other source than Whitman himself, this is a wonderful tableau for any historical mural. Lafayette, who was only twenty years old at the time he served in the American Revolution as Washington's aide, was one of the last surviving Revolutionary heroes. His kissing of the boy Whitman almost has the air of a religious confirmation, a passing on of the spirit of Liberty (p. 397).

• "Abraham Lincoln": Whitman wasn't much for celebrity, but he does make special note of another encounter with a famous person. During the War, Whitman sees President Lincoln "almost every day" as the President travels to work at the White House. Even without the benefit of hindsight, it strikes us as remarkable that a President would be in such close contact with the "man on the street" during wartime. The President was accompanied by a bodyguard, but Whitman assures us that this was against the President's "personal wish." It's especially exciting when Lincoln and Walt Whitman meet, though the encounter may be one of the most reserved introductions ever recorded. As Whitman tells us, once the President's party "passed very close" to where Whitman was standing. "I saw the President in the face fully, as they were moving slowly, and his look, though abstracted, happen'd to be directed steadily in my eye. He bow'd and smiled" (p. 435).

• "The White House by Moonlight": In February, 1863, there was "a spell of fine soft weather" in Washington, D.C., and Whitman wandered down by the White House. The official residence of the President takes on a fantastic, Xanadu-like air as Whitman gazes on "the White House of future poems, and of dreams and dramas, there in the soft and copious moon," while the sentries pace in their overcoats, "stopping you not at all, but eyeing you with sharp eyes, whichever way you move" (p. 418).

• "Spiritual Characters among the Soldiers": Whitman notes that every so often he comes upon a soldier who is blessed with a "strange spiritual sweetness." They are likely to be found in any regiment, from all sections of the country and from every kind of background. Among their comrades their special nature is recognized but vaguely. They are seen as a little "different than the rest," "something odd about them," but what makes them peculiar is not easily identified. Whitman calls them "specimens of unworldliness, disinterestedness, and animal purity and heroism," and says they are "apt to go off and meditate and muse in solitude" (p. 440).

• "Hospital Scenes—Incidents": Though Whitman's war stories come from the hospital and not the battlefield, they have the authentic ring of actual witness. We feel that we have a privileged insight into the war's conditions. Whitman's democratic habit of juxtaposing incidents and observations that seemingly have little to do with each other serves especially well to convey the range of wartime emotion. This group of four incidents includes a random Sunday afternoon in the wards that finds Whitman among a group of critically wounded soldiers; a hot day on which he purchases a large quantity of ice cream and distributes it through the wards; the gruesome incident of the giant rebel soldier wounded in the head so his "brains partially exuded," and a story about Union troops dug in at Columbia, Tennessee, and firing on any wounded Confederate who tried to crawl off the battlefield (p. 447).

• "Southern Escapees": One of the most partisan moments in *Specimen Days* occurs when Whitman refers to Southern deserters as "escapees," while for him Union deserters remain deserters. As the war dragged on and food and clothing supplies for the Southern army began to peter out, more and more conscripts abandoned the Southern army and made their way to the North. Whitman saw gangs of them on the Washington streets, threadbare, exhausted, and bewildered. He imagined that the deserters saw in his face the "pity and fatherliness" that was in his heart, and made the acquaintance of several. One of the "escapees" he befriended was John Wormley of the 9th Alabama, whose parents were both dead. The young soldier wanted only some clean underclothes and a pair of decent pants. He "didn't care about coat or hat fixings." Whitman "had the very great pleasure of helping him to accomplish all those wholesome designs" (p. 458).

• "A Sun-Bath—Nakedness": At the close of *Specimen Days*, Whitman quotes Marcus Aurelius's query on the nature of virtue: "What is it, only a living and enthusiastic sympathy with Nature?" That sympathy is particularly realized in the notes from Timber Creek, where Whitman effected a therapy for his own partial paralysis by wrestling with oak saplings "thick as my wrist" and inventing his own hardy version of taking the baths. Removing all clothing except for his broadbrim straw hat, he takes a stiff brush and rasps his "arms, breast, sides, till they turn'd scarlet." He follows the flesh-brushing with a bath in "the clear waters of the running brook—taking everything very leisurely, with many rests and pauses—stepping about bare-footed every few minutes now and then in some neighboring black ooze, for unctuous mud-bath to my feet—a brief second and third rinsing in the crystal running waters—rubbing with the fragrant towel—slow negligent promenades on the turf up and down in the sun, varied with occasional rests, and further frictions of the bristle-brush—sometimes carrying my portable chair with me from place to place, as my range is quite extensive here, nearly a hundred rods, feeling quite secure from intrusion, (and that indeed I am not at all nervous about, if it accidentally happens)" (p. 512).

• "Spring Overtures—Recreations": While he wrestles the oak saplings, he accompanies his exertions with a range of verbal pipings: "I launch forth in my vocalism: shout declamatory pieces, sentiments, sorrow, anger, &c., from the stock poets or plays—or inflate my lungs and sing the wild tunes and refrains I heard of the blacks down south, or patriotic songs I learn'd in the army. I make the echoes ring, I tell you" (p. 506).

• "Manhattan from the Bay": On June 25, 1878, Whitman

goes for a sail in the bay southeast of Staten Island and returns through New York Harbor. It is a glorious, breezy June day, and as Whitman's boat sails through the harbor he salutes the prospect before him, an exciting amalgam of urban bustle, natural splendor, and the grand, multiplicitous navy that filled the port of New York in the days when most of the world's cargo was shipped by boat. In one epic sentence, his gaze sweeps across the Hudson River and Manhattan island to the East River and the bridge leading to Brooklyn (the Manhattan Bridge), without overlooking the darting boats and birds in his line of sight (p. 530).

• "A Silent Little Fellow—The Coreopsis": Whitman's rhetoric is sometimes overinflated, but there's always another side to him, the side that brings to our attention particulars that no other writer seems to have noticed so keenly. In my discussion of the Western jaunt above, I mention the entry on the coreopsis, a hardy little yellow wildflower that Whitman sees repeatedly throughout that trip. It is remarkable that Whitman, between evocations of a New American Literature and paeans to the Great Plains states and their inhabitants, finds time for this modest flower. But it is even more remarkable that he then recalls all those places in his travels where he has seen the coreopsis, from Lake Champlain to Pike's Peak, with specific references to the places in between (p. 572).

• "Two City Areas, Certain Hours": In May, 1879, in New York, Whitman notices the "brilliant, animated, crowded, spectacular human presentations" in the Union Square area. He is delighted by the prosperous daily crowds of "from thirty to forty thousand finely-dress'd people, all in motion, plenty of them good-looking, many beautiful women, often youths and children, the latter in groups with their nurses." He sees all as display of New York's "countless prodigality of locomotion, dry goods, glitter, magnetism, and happiness" (p. 553).

• "Central Park Walks and Talks": During the week of May 16–22, 1879, Whitman visited New York City's Central Park "almost every day." Here he becomes "friendly and chatty" with a young park policeman, born and raised in New York, who responds to Whitman's questions with details of the life of a New York park policeman. The description doesn't sound all that different from the life of a policeman today: pay is on the low side ($2.40 an hour, seven days a week, eight hours a day), and there are "more risks than one might suppose." And yet "upon the whole, the Park force members like it. They see life, and the excitement keeps them up. . . The worst trouble of the regular Park employee is from malarial fever, chills, and the like" (554).

• "A Specimen Tramp Family": In June, 1878, while staying at John Burroughs's home in Ulster County, New York, Whitman goes out for a drive with his host and another friend. After noting the luxuriance and vitality of the countryside, Whitman adds that they "pass'd quite a number of tramps, singly or in couples." He notices a particular family with whom, had he been alone and on foot, "I should have stopp'd and held confab." Several hours later, returning along the same road, Whitman's party again passes the tramp family near where the family has made camp for the night. The woman is carrying in her arms a "rag-bundled, half-starv'd infant" and trying to sell baskets at houses in the neighborhood. Whitman stops and talks to the woman, then buys all the baskets she is carrying. His friend even goes back with the woman to her encampment to buy another basket. As they drive off, Whitman wonders, "Poor woman— what story was it, out of her fortunes, to account for that inexpressibly scared way, those glassy eyes, and that hollow voice?" (p. 529).

Nine Writing Ideas

• Whitman begins *Specimen Days* as it seems all history begins—with the story of the family. Our oldest epics often begin with a royal lineage (as in the Old Testament). As celebrant of the "average," Whitman begins by tracing both the maternal and paternal sides of his own family back for several generations. Along the way, he provides a fascinating glimpse of life on Long Island in the eighteenth century. What do you know about your family's history? Did they always live on this continent? If not, when did they immigrate? Do you know where they came from, why they came, where they landed? Were they prosperous? Did they continue to move? Why or why not? How many times? Does most of your family live near each other? Do you have family in other states? If your family set down roots in one place, what held them there?

• Whitman has a knack of writing about everything as if measured by the eye of eternity. That is, he sounds as if he's not only talking to the person before him, but to readers generations hence. As a result, his perspectives on people and events are much more generous and less partisan than those of most observers. Write about a contemporary person or event as if writing to someone from a future generation.

• Although Whitman has obviously selected representative samples (or specimens) from his diary instead of including all, there is something about the leisure of his method that is integral to it. Keep a diary, not just of your comings and goings, but of the things that interest you, things that catch your eye in the news, etc.

• In recent years, I've worked in a building on New York's Union Square, one of the two areas of New York that Whitman singled out in May 1879 (in his "Two City Areas, Certain Hours" entry in *Specimen Days*) as an example of the "brilliant, animated, crowded, spectacular human presentations" of New York. During the intervening hundred or so years, Union Square has been largely abandoned by the finely dressed crowds of Whitman's day, who have moved uptown. For many years, it became famous as the rallying site for union meetings and protest marches. Recently, it has become a place for street vendors, workers on lunch hour, a flourishing and grim sidewalk drug market, a smattering of college students, and, very recently, a stream of attractive foreign tourists. Neighborhoods, and even single blocks, in big cities often change character quickly. Can you trace the history and development of a block, a park, or a neighborhood that you're familiar with? Have you always lived in the same neighborhood? Has it changed much since you moved into it? If you live in a small town, the neighborhoods may not change so fast, though they probably have changed considerably since the town's founding. Can you trace the history of your town or a part of it?

• Whitman writes about his trips through Missouri and Kansas to Denver, to Canada, and then, of course, his excursions to Boston and New York. By shaking us out of our routine, travel almost always sharpens our senses. Keep a travel diary the next time you go anywhere, even if it's just across town.

• "What is Nature but change? . . . or humanity . . .but Emotion?" (p. 635). Change is not unique to the United States, but our emphasis on change and its rapidity is an essential and intimate part of the American character. Americans seem to take a quirky, almost mystical delight in how fast the world changes and how hard it is to keep up with it. During Whitman's Western jaunt he delights in how rapidly (eleven years) Kansas has been transformed from the home of the buffalo and migrating Native American tribes to the Golden Belt of American wheat production. Try to imagine what the world, the country, or your city or town will be like in twenty years. Imagine that twenty or thirty years from now you're telling a much younger person about "the old days." What do you think will seem quaint or picturesque?

• Whitman repeatedly predicts that the U.S. will some day include both Canada and Cuba. I'm sure that many Canadians and Cubans of Whitman's time suspected that American invasion or annexation or both were not far off. In our time, we think of America's borders as being much more clearly defined. In Whitman's day, the shape of America was changing every year, much as the borders in Africa are constantly changing today. What do you think might have happened if the U.S. did try to annex Canada or Cuba? If the Secessionists were victorious in the Civil War, what do you think the resulting countries would be like today? Write about what you think the map of the U.S. will look like 25, 50, or 100 years from now.

• Whitman writes and delivers a salute to Thomas Paine in Philadelphia on the 140th anniversary of Paine's birth. Though laudatory, the speech is also defensive in tone. Paine, the author of *Common Sense*, had been one of the great heroes of the American Revolution. But something had happened to society and to Paine's reputation in the 100 years between the Revolution and the time of Whitman's speech to make Whitman think that he had to defend Paine. Can you think of a contemporary politician or celebrity whose reputation will be very different in 150 years than it is today? Why do you think that will be so?

• Except for a brief period in his youth, Whitman was not a political activist, though as a newspaper editor he was always ready to take a stand on a controversial issue. He writes in *Democratic Vistas*, "The eager and often inconsiderate appeals of reformers and revolutionists are indispensable, to counterbalance the inertness and fossilism making so large a part of human institutions ... The former are to be treated with indulgence, and even with respect" (p. 338). What do you think Whitman means when he calls these appeals "eager and inconsiderate"? Write about some modern "reformers and revolutionists" who annoy or even weary you, but whom you respect nonetheless.

Writing Civil War Ballads from Photographs and Whitman's Words

by Margot Fortunato Galt

In this exercise, my students and I write modern ballads based on photographs of Civil War scenes and Walt Whitman's writings about the war. The combination of visual and literary sources brings us close to the Civil War's particular combination of casual grime and impassioned rhetoric. This two-day exercise works well with high school students. It encourages them to consider how the war's photographic record, the first extensive one of its kind, differs from Whitman's literary portrait of the war.

Photographs brought the Civil War home to the civilian population. Calling-card portraits of soldiers and battle scenes for stereopticon viewers sold by the millions. Through engravings based on photographs, the nineteenth-century newspapers and magazines carried the war into people's parlors with almost as much force as TV brought Vietnam into our living rooms.

At first the photographs of any war remind viewers of the particular conflict. But gradually the pictures of wars become universal—we see death in a ditch rather than the Civil War's complicated reality of slavery, broken families, primitive medicine (by our standards), and the threatened Union and impoverished South. Soon, if they haven't already, even the images of Vietnam may evoke not the Gulf of Tonkin incident, the My Lai massacre, Kansas boys fighting in rice paddies, or R & R in Hong Kong, but war in general.

Written records age differently. Over time, they seem more and more imbued with the spirit, and technology, and everyday objects of a particular war. Walt Whitman's poems and reports from Civil War battlefields and hospitals are filled with the roar of cannons, the flap of flags, the clank of men marching, the groans of the wounded and amputees. Whitman uses terms that sound both archaic and accurate. He writes about dying with an unflinching, almost contemporary show of pain and gore, and about death with a sweetness that seems faded, but true to his time. His words bring our particular Civil War to mind, real, historical, and distant. In some passages, where the historical predominates over the eternal, we might even forget the universal qualities of war, the pain, squalor and dislocation, and be tempted to romanticize the Civil War, imagining it to be a sort of pageant with historically accurate replicas of neat uniforms, mess kits, and hospital tents, and none of the disease and death that so characterized it.

That's where we need to bring in the photographs, the careful studies of camp soldiers, ruined cities, ditches of Rebel and Union dead. Mathew Brady, Alexander Gardner, and others documented the Civil War with painstaking precision. Their photographs are static, but they have a physical solidity we have to believe could have been pictured yesterday.

The often casual intimacy of these photographs is partly the result of the camera's insistent realism, but also occurs because the photographers documented the common soldiers, not just the generals in heroic studio poses. Like many of Whitman's poems and prose reports from the battlefields, Civil War photographs have an offhand starkness and humor about them. We tell ourselves that the moments shown have passed, but we do not doubt that they occurred and that the soldiers felt fatigue, terror, and loneliness.

Taken alone, the photos tend to remind us of our recent wars—whether it be World War II, Korea, Vietnam, or, to a lesser extent, the Gulf. Combining the Civil War photographs with Whitman's writings helps us acknowledge what makes the Civil War seem archaic and past. Taken with Whitman's words, the photographs help us enter the experience of the past.

Advance Preparation: Selecting Passages from Whitman and Finding Civil War Photographs

Before beginning this exercise, I read poems and prose reports that Whitman wrote about the Civil War and then select passages to read aloud to the students. If time permits, the students can read from Whitman's work in the "Drum Taps" section of *Leaves of Grass*, and in the prose collection called *Specimen Days*. Then, on their own, the students can choose poems and prose to read aloud to each other. (Much of Whitman's Civil War work appears in *The Portable Walt Whitman*, edited by Mark Van Doren [New York: Penguin, 1973].)

The stereograph photographs that I use with this exercise are xerox copies of rectangular, cardboard-backed stereopticon slides that were often sold as sets to the nineteenth-century viewers. Inserted into the holder of the stereopticon, the double images of the slides merged into one and gave the illusion of depth, like 3-D movies. Buying a set was probably comparable to renting a video today—any middle-class family of the time could do it.

But stereograph photos hardly exhaust the possible photographic record of the war. Many photographs were made for newspapers and magazines or for the soldiers to give as mementos before they went to battle. Perhaps the most easily available modern publications of the whole range of Civil War photographs are the two series by Time-Life Books, *The Civil War* and *The Image of War*. Many photographs have also been duplicated in the lengthy and informative PBS television series "The Civil War," produced by Ken Burns.

In the Time-Life books, photographs are labeled with helpful information. For example, in the volume called *Tenting Tonight* (by James I. Robertson, Jr., in the *Civil War* series, 1984), one photograph carries this caption: "Men of the 1st Texas Brigade engage in a variety of chores—scrubbing clothes, frying corn pone and chopping firewood—outside their winter quarters at Camp Quantico, Virginia in 1861. The log hut was opulent by army standards, featuring a roof of sturdy shingles and a glass window with nearly every pane intact" (p. 12). If you are short on time or information, the Time-Life volumes will prove especially helpful.

But finding local collections of photos at state or country historical societies also has its advantages. The local collections add an immediacy to the writing experience—after all, the Civil War touched nearly every part of the nation. With individual photos, it is also possible to make xeroxed copies for students without too much expense.

Identifying the photos from historical societies need not be difficult. On each stereopticon slide, for example, a short printed phrase describes the scene and more elaborate text appears on the back. If you want more information, a good reference book is *The Civil War Dictionary* by Mark M. Boatner III. The Time-Life series also contains many descriptions of particular battles, sieges, regiments, officers, and fighting men.

Fig. 3: Professor Lowe in his balloon watching the battle of Fair Oaks, Peninsula Campaign, 1862. Courtesy of the Minnesota Historical Society.

Fig. 4: "Where One of Grant's Messengers Called," 1865, stereopticon slide. When looked at through a stereopticon viewer, these two slightly different views of the same scene appeared to be three dimensional.

Fig. 5: "Savage's Station," June 29, 1862.

When I leafed through the collection of stereopticon slides and other photographs at the Minnesota Historical Society, I selected a variety of shots, fifteen in all. Here are the label information and notes on some:

• "Professor Lowe in His Balloon, from the 1862 Peninsula Campaign" (fig. 3). From the back I took the following notes: Army balloon aided signal service. The Fair Oaks Battle: the balloon followed the enemy's movements and gave warning to the generals on how to head them off. Men holding the ropes permitted the balloon to rise, then anchored it to a tree.

• "The Sunken Road at Antietam." Notes indicate that this ditch was used by Rebels as a rifle pit. The Union battery got excellent range of the road and slaughtered the enemy like sheep. The dead were photographed where they fell. (Research has uncovered the fact that occasionally the Civil War photographers repositioned dead soldiers in beatific poses and even put crosses in their hands, but this slide is labeled specifically, "the dead were photographed where they fell.")

• "Where One of Grant's Messengers Called," a stereopticon slide (fig. 4). I noted: the city of Petersburg, Virginia, was under fire from July 1864–April 1865. The Union batteries shelled almost continuously, yet many women and children stayed in Petersburg during the seige. The photo shows the Dunlop house from inside a dim, plaster-littered parlor, looking out of a shattered window. "Grant's Messenger" was obviously a cannon ball.

• "Savage's Station, 1862" (fig. 5). From the back I noted: A crowd of sick and wounded from the 1st Minnesota Regiment spread beside a railroad station under a tree and ladder. June 29, 1862. The Richmond and York River railroad tracks ran nearby.

Day One

Except for advanced students, this Civil War ballad exercise takes two days, with brainstorming and note-taking occupying the first day, and modeling and writing the second.

Step One: Choosing a Partner and a Photograph

The first time I tried this Civil War ballad exercise, I worked with a group of eleventh-grade humanities students who had just read Stephen Crane's novel about the Civil War, *The Red Badge of Courage*. I have also tried it with twelfth-grade English students, who had not studied the war.

Ideally, the students should have done some reading about the war before they try writing from photographs. Dipping into the Time-Life *Civil War* books or seeing some of the PBS "Civil War" series would be good preparation for understanding some of the minutiae that made this war different from all others—the cornmeal, hardtack, minnie ball, cannons, horse-drawn covered wagons, songs, slang.

After this preparation, the students choose partners and select a photograph to examine together.

Step Two: Describing the Poem for the Students

To help the students envision the whole course of the project, I describe the kind of poem we aim to create: a ballad, with choruses alternating with descriptive verses. The lines for the choruses can come, in part, from Whitman's poetry and prose. The lines in the verses will come from the students' responses to the photographs, bringing out the details and the drama that the students find in them.

Each pair of writers can decide whether to create both chorus and verses together, or whether one writer will write the verses and the other the chorus. I suggest to them that the chorus can change slightly to indicate a deepening of the poem's meaning.

Later we will read Whitman's "Beat! Beat! Drums!" as an example of a poem whose chorus becomes more complex as the poem moves toward conclusion.

Step Three: Questioning the Image, Defining the Scene

I ask the students to work in pairs because deciphering the visual details in the faded photographs can be difficult. As one student asks questions about the image, the other can put into words what the photo shows. Questions and answers, especially when written down, are a valuable form of brainstorming. I encourage the teams to add imagination to the realistic details in the photographs, and also to incorporate information they have gleaned about the war. The questions and answers about the image of "Savage's Station—1862" might go something like this:

Question: "Why is there a ladder slanting across the picture to the upstairs of Savage's Station?"

Answer: "Maybe because there are wounded men upstairs and the inside stairway has been burned out."

Question: "What do you think is happening inside the tent on the outskirts of the crowd of wounded?"

Answer: "Maybe it's a cook tent or maybe the doctor performs surgery there."

Included in the process of question and answer are simple descriptions of what is visible in the photograph. I urge everyone to look for details that characterize a place or a person: "Notice the man with the wide-brimmed straw hat hunched in the foreground. He doesn't look very sick, just exhausted and discouraged." Or, "The white picket fence around the mass of wounded men looks incongruous—this is hardly a pretty garden with flowers in it anymore."

I encourage the students to write down anything they know that they might bring to bear on the photograph; for instance, "With only ether and chloroform and no antibiotics, the pain of surgery and the danger of infection must have been great."

A partner might respond, "I can imagine the air heavy with the smell of sweat and blood. The scene looks almost idyllic in black and white, but screams are probably coming from the surgeon's tent. When gangrene set in, the doctor could only amputate." Then we might say, "The bodies are so close together, there is no privacy, but that probably doesn't matter. With so much pain, you stop caring where you are or who hears you cry out."

In other words, a close examination of the photos helps the students *get inside* them.

It also helps to ask, "What is about to happen next?" We know that the scenes captured in photos are present only for a moment before they alter. Trying to imagine what will happen next may help the students draw on their knowledge of the war. Of Savage's Station, we might guess, "As soon as the camera clicks, a train will pull in and then will come the long process of moving the wounded into flatcars for transportation to the hospitals in Washington."

Step Four: Note-Taking from Whitman

The "Drum Taps" section of *Leaves of Grass* forms the core of Whitman's poetry about the war. His prose reports, more heavily grained, casual and hurried, were often published in New York newspapers or later collected in his *Specimen Days*.

Whitman spent more than three years, from late 1862 through 1865, following the Army of the Potomac. Much of the time he stayed in Washington visiting and nursing sick and wounded soldiers, but he also "went down to the fields in Virginia (end of '62); lived thenceforward in camp; saw great battles and the days and nights afterward; partook of all the fluctuations, gloom, despair, hopes again aroused, courage evoked, death readily risked. . . ." (p. 12 in Walter Lowenfels's 1960 compilation *Walt Whitman's Civil War*, which includes war reports that are not reprinted in *The Portable Walt Whitman*).

Much of the prose and the poems from "Drum Taps" that I use in class come from *The Portable Walt Whitman*, from which I select passages to read aloud. I prefer reading aloud because it's a better way for us to take in the rich language and long cadences of Whitman's writing.

As we listen, we are struck by vivid and telling phrases. I have the students write these phrases down to use later as the beginning of the chorus to a poem, especially the phrases that seem to relate to the photo they've chosen. The idea isn't just to mimic Whitman whole hog, but rather to absorb the precise terms of this one war and to enrich our own description of the photographs with Whitman's unmatched range and sensitivity.

So I direct the class to take notes as I read the prose and poems aloud. I ask everyone to do this because though their poems will be a joint effort, individual responses will contribute variety to the final product.

To give a sense of how the war initially felt to a civilian, I often begin with a section of the first poem from "Drum-Taps," "First O Songs for a Prelude" (in the Penguin *Complete Poems*, ed. Francis Murphy, 1989):

To the drum-taps prompt,
The young men falling in and arming,
The mechanics arming, (the trowel, the jack-plane, the blacksmith's
    hammer, tost aside with precipitation,)
The lawyer leaving his office and arming, the judge leaving the court,
The driver deserting his wagon in the street, jumping down, throwing
    the reins abruptly down on the horses' backs,
The salesman leaving the store, the boss, book-keeper, porter, all
    leaving;
Squads gather everywhere by common consent and arm,
The new recruits, even boys, the old men show them how to wear their

accoutrements, they buckle the straps carefully,
Outdoors arming, indoors arming, the flash of musket-barrels,
The white tents cluster in camps, the arm'd sentries around, the sunrise
    cannon and again at sunset,
Arm'd regiments arrive every day, pass through the city, and embark
    from the wharves, [. . .]
The tearful parting, the mother kisses her son, the son kisses his
    mother, [. . .]
The artillery, the silent cannons bright as gold, drawn along, rumble
    lightly over the stones, . . .
The hospital service, the lint, bandages and medicines,
The women volunteering for nurses, the work begun for in earnest, no
    more parade now [...]

I then read the stirring ballad "Beat! Beat! Drums!":

Beat! beat! drums—blow! bugles! blow!
Through the windows—through doors—burst like a ruthless force,
Into the solemn church, and scatter the congregation,
Into the school where the scholar is studying;
Leave not the bridegroom quiet—no happiness must he have now with
    his bride,
Nor the peaceful farmer any peace, ploughing his field or gathering his
    grain,
So fierce you whirr and pound you drums—so shrill you bugles blow.

Beat! beat! drums!—blow! bugles! blow
Over the traffic of cities—over the rumble of wheels in the streets;
Are beds prepared for sleepers at night in the houses? no sleepers must
    sleep in those beds,
No bargainers' bargains by day—no brokers or speculators—would
    they continue?
Would the talkers be talking? would the singer attempt to sing?
Would the lawyer rise in the court to state his case before the judge?
Then rattle quicker, heavier drums—you bugles wilder blow.

Beat! beat! drums!—blow! bugles! blow!
Make no parley—stop for no expostulation,
Mind not the timid—mind not the weeper or prayer,
Mind not the old man beseeching the young man,
Let not the child's voice be heard, not the mother's entreaties,
Make even the trestles to shake the dead where they lie awaiting the
    hearses,
So strong you thump O terrible drums—so loud you bugles blow.

Before moving on, I point out the changes in the chorus to emphasize the growing effect of the war.

After being aroused with Whitman's battle calls, we next follow him to the Virginia battlefields in a prose selection from *Specimen Days* (in *The Portable Whitman*, pp. 411–412). Notice how the details here echo the subject in the photo of "Savage's Station":

Down at the Front
Falmouth, Va., opposite Fredericksburg, December 21, 1862.
—Began my visits among the camp hospitals in the army of the Potomac. Spend a good part of the day in a large brick mansion on the banks of the Rappahannock, used as a hospital since the battle—seems to have receiv'd only the worst cases. Out doors, at the foot of a tree, within ten yards of the front of the house, I notice a heap of amputated feet, legs, arms, hands, &c., a full load for a one-horse cart. Several dead bodies lie near, each cover'd with its brown woolen blanket. In the dooryard, towards the river, are fresh graves, mostly of officers, their names on pieces of barrel-staves or broken boards stuck in the dirt. [. . .] The large mansion is quite crowded upstairs and down, everything impromptu, no system, all bad enough, but I have no doubt the best that can be done; all the wounds pretty bad, some frightful, the men in their old clothes, unclean and bloody. [. . .] I went through the rooms, downstairs and up. Some of the men were dying. I had nothing to give at that visit, but wrote a few letters to folks home, mothers, &c. Also talk'd to three or four, who seemed most susceptible to it, and needing it.

The contrast between the mood of the poetry and that of the prose is striking. Whitman's heroic poems heighten individual resolve into an immense, democratic contribution. They do not focus so much on the grimy, mean, and accidental elements of war that his prose steadily records.

Expressing Whitman's noble version of the Union, the poems frame the war's brutality with images from soothing nature, such as the haunting motifs of lilacs, evening star, and the hermit thrush's "song of the bleeding throat" from "When Lilacs Last in the Dooryard Bloom'd." But in the prose, though he tries to make a new moon "prove an omen and a good prophecy," such hope and comfort don't always carry into his description of the dirt and pain of battle.

In a paragraph on the battle of Fredericksburg, Sunday, 14 December 1862, Whitman describes an exhausting attack:

During the whole of that time [twenty-seven hours of attack], everyone, from the Colonel on down, was compelled to lie at full length on his back or belly in the mud, which was deep and tenacious. The surface of the ground, slightly elevated just south of them, served as a natural bulwark and protection against the Rebel batteries and sharpshooters, as long as the men lay in this manner. But the moment the men raised their heads or a limb, even if only a few inches—snap and s-s-st went the weapons of Secesh! In this manner, the 51st remained spread out in the mud all Sunday night, all Monday and Monday night till after midnight. Although the troops could plainly hear the Rebels whistling, etc., the latter did not dare advance upon them.

Even when the scene is a quiet day in camp, Whitman does not ennoble the soldiers; he describes them with the passion of an attentive draftsman:

Nearby was the camp of the 26th Pennsylvania, who have been out since the commencement of the war. I talked with a couple of the men, part of a squad around a fire, in the usual enclosure of green branches fencing three sides of a space perhaps twenty feet square—breaking the wind from north and east. Where there are boughs to be had, these sylvan corrals are to be met with in all the camps, some of them built very finely and making a picturesque appearance for a camp. They serve as the company kitchens and the same purpose of rendezvous of an evening that the public house, the reading room, or the engine house did at home. . . .

The tents of this camp were quite comfortable, such moderate weather as we are having now [December 1862]. One of the men came out of a tent close by, with a couple of slices of beef and some crackers, and commenced cooking the mess in a frying pan for his breakfast. It looked very good. Another man was waiting with similar articles to have the use of the frying pan. . . .

I thought, rough as it was, that men in health might endure it and get along with more comfort than most outsiders would suppose—as indeed the condition of the men around me was tolerable proof.

The mass of our men in our army are young; it is an impressive sight to me to see the countless number of youths and boys. There is only a sprinkling of elderly men. On a parade at evening there you see them, poor lads, many of them already with the experience of the oldest veterans. (Lowenfels, pp. 36–37)

Next I read an 1865 poem from "Drum-Taps." Whitman's sympathy for the young soldiers wounded and dying in battle fills the rhythmic, compelling lines of this poem titled from its first line:

A march in the ranks hard-prest, and the road unknown,
A route through a heavy wood with muffled steps in the darkness,
Our army foil'd with loss severe, and the sullen remnant retreating,
Till after midnight glimmer upon us the lights of a dim-lighted building,
'Tis a large old church at the crossing-roads, now an impromptu hospital,
Entering but for a minute I see a sight beyond all the pictures and poems ever made,
Shadows of deepest, deepest black, just lit by moving candles and lamps,
And by one great pitchy torch stationary with wild red flame and clouds of smoke,
By these, crowds, groups of forms vaguely I see on the floor, some in the pews laid down,
At my feet more distinctly a soldier, a mere lad, in danger of bleeding to death, (he is shot in the abdomen,)
I stanch the blood temporarily, (the youngster's face is white as a lily,)
Then before I depart I sweep my eyes o'er the scene fain to absorb it all
[. . .]
Then hear outside the orders given, *Fall in, my men, fall in*;
But first I bend to the dying lad, his eyes open a half-smile gives he me.
Then the eyes close, calmly close, and I speed forth to the darkness,
Resuming, marching, ever in darkness marching, on in the ranks,
The unknown road still marching.

Students often note the following phrases: "the road unknown," "shadows of deepest, deepest black," "wild red flame," "a mere lad in danger of bleeding to death," and "face is white as a lily." Whitman's contrast of light and dark reflects his own extreme emotion, suddenly brought to bear on the dying youth. And the lily he sees in the young face sanctifies this death in the midst of the "smell of ether, the odor of blood." The face "white as a lily" suggests a hope for resurrection. Whitman finds a war that is modern in its slaughter and size, but because he is living in the nineteenth century, he is not inured to such senseless destruction: he requires some meaning for the sacrifice.

Day Two

For the best continuity, the second day of the exercise should immediately follow the first.

Step Six: Fashioning the Poem

The first thing we do is put together the choruses for the poems. Depending on the students' experience, they either start writing immediately or I do a demonstration on the board, using Whitman's phrases suggested by members of the class. When it is hard to decide how much of Whitman's language to use in a line, or when to alter it to fit our purposes, a demonstration can model some strategies. To do this, I ask class members to swap notes with each other and then to read out phrases they like. Let's imagine that from this we have collected the following phrases on the board:

by common consent and arm
musketry so general
on in the ranks
a ruthless force
flash of musket barrels
sunrise cannon and one at sunset
one great pitchy torch
in pews laid down
full length in mud
dare advance
youths with the experience of oldest veterans
face white as a lily
several dead bodies lay near
men in old clothes and are dirty
leave not the bridegroom quiet
at my feet a soldier, a mere lad
at the foot of the tree, amputated feet, arms, hands
no happiness must he have with his bride
the mass of men in the army are young
men dying upstairs and down
no sleepers must sleep in those beds
heap of amputated limbs
our army foiled with severe loss
orders given to fall in
27 hours of attack . . . everyone lying on their backs

so shrill you bugles blow
fresh graves of mostly officers
shadows of deepest, deepest black
names on barrel boards stuffed in the dust
the eyes calmly closed in death

Playing around with the phrases—condensing and rear-ranging them, for instance—leads us to some unusual combinations:

Flash of sunrise cannon.
Youths dare advance.
White as a lily
in pews laid down.

or

Youths the highest veterans
consent and arm.
One great pitchy torch
full length in the mud.

The lines of these choruses use standard poetic lengths of between four and seven syllables. But after reading Whitman, we know that much longer, sweeping lines are possible. Make a shape that suits you, I tell the students. If you want to try long lines, add your own words to the phrases you've taken from Whitman.

The chorus may also come from our own words and ideas. We can look to Whitman for historical details, then cast them in our own words. Either way, the chorus can evoke the essence of the photograph.

The verses can relate a short narrative of events suggested by the photograph. The narrative can be fairly simple, with the photo recording one moment in the narrative. Each verse can disclose a bit more of the imagined events about imaginary characters in the narrative. The chorus then comments on the underlying mood and meaning of the developing narrative.

Even with the extensive preparation, students sometimes have trouble getting started. In that case, I read aloud several Civil War ballads by other students to show them how the choruses and verses can work together. These poems describe some of the same photographs the present class is using, which also helps the writers move from brainstorming to drafting. Good student examples are included below.

Once the students start writing, they usually need thirty minutes to draft a full poem. As they work, I move around the classroom to answer questions. Sometimes I help students decipher a photograph or refer them to a section of a reference book. I also remind them of a strategy we mentioned: altering the chorus to indicate a change in the narrative. Students also try out ideas on me as they begin to enter the lives of the people in the photographs. I encourage them to invent people who are not shown, such as a family for the Dunlop House in Petersburg, or a wife or mother at home to whom a soldier might be writing.

As the writing emerges, students often show me what they have so far. I respond by emphasizing what I like, occasionally correcting modern slang that seems out of place, or suggesting what could happen next. The students sometimes ask to see the other student examples I have read to them, to check the shape of the poems and refresh their memories of content.

Student Examples

The following poems by eleventh-grade humanities students are fine examples of the brief evocative narratives and choruses the photographs can inspire. The first poem below, titled "First Minnesota Squad—After Fair Oaks," refers to a picture of a cannon looming in the foreground. In the midground, men stand idly by, with timbers and carts strewn around them. In the distance an old frame house seems to survey the quiet of the field where 400 men were buried after battle.

First Minnesota Squad—After Fair Oaks

Steel cannon lie silent,
Helpless in the aftermath,
No comfort for mourners.

Under cloudless skies
Docile cows wander.
Frame house stands silent,
Looking upon the morbid scene.

Immune from this disease of war.

Lone soldier prays,
"End this hell of pain."
Distant soldier strays:
the frame house speaks of home.

Under cloudless skies
Docile cows wander.
Frame house stands silent,
Looking upon the morbid scene.
Immune from this disease of war.

The cold, hard ground
Houses cold, decaying bodies.
Over four hundred perished.
   —*Christina Seagren and Bridget DeFrank*

Another poem, by high school students Bill Shepherd and Dave
Barden, is from the photograph of the besieged Dunlop House in
Petersburg, Virginia, 1864.

What Might Have Been

Through a broken window
Past shattered shards of glass
Lies a blurry image
Of what might have been.

Guns sound. Union army.
The shelling has begun.
First one hits. Buildings shake.
Fear spreads through the town.

Through a broken window
Past shattered shards of glass
Lies a blurry image
Of what might have been.

Broken bricks, fire blazing.
Faint sound heard, child crying.
Loud he cries, no one hears
Till death claims its prey.

Through a broken window
Past shattered shards of glass
Lies a blurry image
Of what might have been.

Cannons stop. Night has come.
Dog whimpers. Master fears.
Woman stands by the glass.
Looking out at death.

Through a broken window,
Past shattered shards of glass,
Lies a blurry image
Of what should have been.

The choruses in these poems are composed of the students' own words. They divided up the work, with one responsible for the verses and the other for the choruses. I like the way the one-word change in the last line emphasizes the poignancy of the family who have watched their house collapse around them.

In another set of poems written by eleventh- and twelfth-grade students, the choruses are composed of Whitman's own words. The poem below is based on a group photo of men in front of the standard Union camp tent called the "Sibley tent," which housed around fifteen men:

Twenty-Four Hours to Attack

The mass of men in the army are young.
Men in old clothes that are dirty.
Orders given to fall in, twenty-four hours to attack.
The youngster's face white as a lily.

Like the sick man standing in back
too proud to lie on his back
when his country needs him,
patriotic, though facing death.

The mass of men in the army are young,
Men in old clothes that are dirty.
Orders given to fall in, twenty hours to attack.
The youngster's face white as a lily.

Unlike the bearded man,
a veteran of many battles,
nonchalantly sharpening his knife.
Waiting, preparing for battle.

The mass of men in the army are young.
Men in old clothes that are dirty.
Orders given to fall in, sixteen hours to attack.
The youngster's face white as a lily.

The artist, drawing the men,
silent, not wanting to break
the quiet meditating of the troops.
Wondering if he is sketching already dead men.

The mass of men in the army are young.
Men in old clothes that are dirty.
Orders given to fall in, eight hours to attack.
The youngster's face white as a lily.

The youngster, not yet having seen "the elephant"
writes out a will, mailing it home.
Scared to die.
But will for his country.

The mass of men in the army are young.
Men in old clothes that are dirty.
Orders given to fall in, zero hours to attack.
The youngster's face white as a lily.

The battle is over.
The Yankees are victorious.
The Rebels in retreat.
The survivors gather around the flag.

The mass of men in the army are young.
Men in old clothes that are dirty.
Orders given to fall in, twenty-four hours to attack.
The youngster's face, grim with determination.
        —*Tom Pesta, Joe Lounsbery, and Pat Nesburg*

These students have created choruses to indicate the count-
down to battle, and then in the last line of the chorus they change

the fearful youth with face "white as a lily" to a youth "grim with determination" after he has fought a battle.

In the following poem, students describe the destruction of a Virginia landmark and suggest the failure of secessionist rhetoric. Again, the chorus is drawn from Whitman's phrases, with additions and changes by the students.

Chambersburg Court House

So shrill you bugles blow,
your tone riddles my bare bones.
Several dead bodies lie near
their eyes closed, calmly closed.
Twenty-seven hours of attack
stripped years upon years away.
Blow you bugles blow.

Men, brave, arrogant men
once filled these walls —
cries of war
boast of victory
bounced from stone to stone,
memories of their forefathers
etched deep in my bones.

So shrill you bugles blow,
your tone riddles my bare bones.
Several dead bodies lie near
their eyes closed, calmly closed.
Twenty-seven hours of attack
stripped years upon years away.
Blow you bugles blow.

A crack of thunder,
cannons roared.
I stood in pain
weeping.
Feelings, memories drift like smoke
from under my crumpled skin.
The voices heard no more,
the wind is chilling,
death predominant.

So shrill you bugles blow,
your tone riddles my bare bones.
Several dead bodies lie near,
their eyes closed, calmly closed.
Twenty-seven hours of attack
stripped years upon years away.
Blow you bugles blow.

Years gone by.
A child stumbles through my remains.
He gazes in wonder
at my exposed flesh.
He would never know me
or understand my past—
the boasts of men
turned to ghosts
lost.

So shrill you bugles blow,
your tone riddles my bare bones.
The dead bodies are gone,
their eyes closed calmly forever.
Twenty-seven hours of attack
stripped my existence away.
Blow you bugles blow.
　　　—Brian Young and Kate Terwey

These students' description of the attack is rather general until the last stanza, but by the end they themselves have gone through the harrowing business of identifying with the fighting men. The attack has "stripped my existence away," they write, testifying to the power of the imagination to recreate war's bloodshed and death.

Writing poetry about the Civil War requires the writer to bridge the distance between now and then. After the exercise, students have commented that they thought more closely about the possibility of war in their own time just as I had thought of Vietnam. When we study history at arm's length, with more emphasis on facts than on individual human responses, such connections are not as likely to happen. The past remains manageable and does not get under our skin.

But when we invite imagination to enter our study of history, we open the door to character, emotion, irony, and the magic of metaphorical language. We identify individuals, as do the three authors of "Twenty-Four Hours to Attack": the proud, sick patriot; the veteran who "nonchalantly sharpens his knife"; the artist already sensing death on the countenances of his subjects; and finally the youth who writes his will before his first battle. Once individuals enter the stage of history, we can't pretend that the story concerns a faceless group; we become aware of diversity and of our responsibility to judge carefully any generalization about past or present peoples.

We also recognize that the Civil War, like all wars, affected people whose stories have remained private, not recorded in any form we can unearth. In the poem about the Dunlop House, the students have allowed imagination to enter a Virginia house with a family who become believable because their responses strike familiar emotions. When a dog whimpers, a master fears, and a woman stands at the window looking at death, we understand that history takes time, that destruction occurs over months in people's lives. We can then begin to measure not only the physical toll but also a psychological one.

Through metaphor and irony, the students convey the terrible price of war, the shallowness of its boasts, the extent of its destruction. "Immune from this disease of war," write Christina Seagren and Bridget DeFrank, and, by comparing war to a disease, suggest how hard it is for any individual to escape infection. The "cries of war/boast of victory" that Brian Young and Kate Terwey imagine in the Southern courthouse soon etch deep in dead bones an inheritance of egotism and slavery far from the orator's bold intentions.

Whitman's rich and evocative language helps the students to realize in their own writing the power of irony and metaphor. Notice how Brian Young and Kate Terwey link Whitman's "So shrill you bugles blow" to another metaphor: "Your tone riddles my dead bones," suggesting either the riddle of an unanswerable question, or bullets striking a body. Whitman's flourishes of patriotic imagery, mixed with his sensitive description of destruction, provide a strong model for the students and help them bring facts together with their own creative use of language. That they are more ironic than Whitman indicates the years that separate him from us, and the difficulty many of us now have of imagining a just cause for war. Under the surface of our poems about the past lie our own attitudes: as we write about history we discover ourselves.

Poems Based on "This Compost"

by Jack Collom

When students are studying ecology, Walt Whitman's poem "This Compost" can bring some fresh air to the subject.

Any good poem resembles a biosystem in that its survival depends on the interrelationships of its parts—on context. A good poem seems to us "a world in itself." The poet weaves with words a network of semblances and distinctions, as nature does. One of Walt Whitman's famous remarks is: "Do I contradict myself? Very well, I contradict myself. I am large; I contain multitudes." Whitman recognizes, and brings us to recognize, that it's only natural to combine forces that, according to any simplistic notion, don't combine. In "This Compost," Whitman combines rot and beauty, death and life, but expressed in terms of immediate facts rather than abstractions.

In the text of the poem below, I've marked my own favorite lines. Read the poem aloud to your class; if you feel like emphasizing the rhythm and energy, go ahead.

This Compost

1.
Something startles me where I thought I was the safest,*
I withdraw from the still woods I loved,
I will not go now on the pastures to walk,
I will not strip the clothes from my body to meet my lover the sea,
I will not touch my flesh to the earth as to other flesh to renew me.

O how can it be that the ground itself does not sicken?
How can you be alive you growths of spring?
How can you furnish health you blood of herbs, roots, orchards, grain?
Are they not continually putting distemper'd corpses within you?*
Is not every continent work'd over and over with sour dead?*

Where have you disposed of their carcasses?
Those drunkards and gluttons of so many generations?
Where have you drawn off all the foul liquid and meat?

I do not see any of it upon you to-day, or perhaps I am deceiv'd.
I will run a furrow with my plough, I will press my spade through the
   sod and turn it up underneath,
I am sure I shall expose some of the foul meat.*

2.
Behold this compost! behold it well!
Perhaps every mite has once form'd part of a sick person—yet behold!*
The grass of spring covers the prairies,
The bean bursts noiselessly through the mould in the garden,*
The delicate spear of the onion pierces upward,
The apple-buds cluster together on the apple-branches,
The resurrection of the wheat appears with pale visage out of its
   graves,*
The tinge awakes over the willow-tree and the mulberry-tree,
The he-birds carol mornings and evenings while the she-birds sit in
   their nests,
The young of poultry break through the hatch'd eggs,
The new-born of animals appear, the calf is dropt from the cow, the colt
   from the mare,
Out of its little hill faithfully rise the potato's dark green leaves,*
Out of its hill rises the yellow maize-stalk, the lilacs bloom in the
   dooryards,
The summer growth is innocent and disdainful above all those strata of
   sour dead.

What chemistry!*
That the winds are really not infectious,
That this is no cheat, this transparent green-wash of the sea which is
   so amorous after me,*
That it is safe to allow it to lick my naked body all over with its tongues,
That it will not endanger me with the fevers that have deposited
   themselves in it,
That all is clean forever and forever,*
That the cool drink from the well tastes so good,
That blackberries are so flavorous and juicy,
That the fruits of the apple-orchard and the orange-orchard, that
   melons, grapes, peaches, plums, will none of them poison me,
That when I recline on the grass I do not catch any disease,
Though probably every spear of grass rises out of what was once a
   catching disease.

Now I am terrified at the Earth, it is that calm and patient,*
It grows such sweet things out of such corruptions,

175

It turns harmless and stainless on its axis, with such endless succes-
sions of diseas'd corpses,*
It distills such exquisite winds out of such infused fetor,
It renews with such unwitting looks its prodigal, annual, sumptuous
crops,
It gives such divine materials to men, and accepts such leavings from
them at last.*

The poem begins with nameless fear; then we find the cause:
the foulness and decay that feeds the earth. But Whitman lets
"melons, grapes, peaches, plums" grow out of it, "and all is clean
forever and forever."

Note Whitman's long, rolling lines (the nineteenth-century
English poet Gerard Manley Hopkins called his work "prose
bewitched"). In the way he combines prose qualities and poetry,
basic fact and strange music, his writing is like nature—full of
surprises, not oversimplified. Point out some of his most unusual
or strongly expressed lines and phrases to your class.

The central shock of the poem is that life rises out of
"ugliness." However, Whitman doesn't start the poem with big
ideas. He shows us emotion and the *things* it connects with; then
and only then he lets the ideas arise, out of these details. Poets
usually work like this — from the thing to the thought, not vice versa.

You might also want to discuss Whitman's fear (of natural
poisons) and its relation to our own present-day fears (of poisons
of our own making).

Have your students write a poem in free verse, not necessarily in Whitman's style, based on some harshness, threat, or
"corruption" in nature. Perhaps their poems can "rise," as "This
Compost" does, to praise nature, but this should never be forced,
and need not happen at all. Or it can be expressed in some tiny
image, left unexplained.

Collect and read aloud, or ask the students to read their own.

Compost-based Poems
(Examples from college-age students)

Death Bed

They crawl
     further in
     deeper and deeper

He yells in disappointment
Her face turns in tears

They crawl
     further in
     deeper and deeper

His first novel is published
She graduates from Law School

They crawl
     further in
     deeper and deeper

A slave is shot through the head
A woman scratches and screams she is being raped

They crawl
     further in
     deeper and deeper

A child is born on New Year's Day
A nation is set free in triumph

They crawl
     further in
     deeper and deeper

I step and the knife blade pierces my boot
A child runs laughing into the street to meet his death

They crawl
     further in
     deeper and deeper

She's on her death bed
      Certain in her faith

A mouse
Lies on the ground

Beside a trail

Dead a couple of days

If you look closer
You see several insects
Maybe the size of moths

Crawling all over
Crawling into
      This mouse

Burrowing and burrowing
Into the back of its head

Digging deep inside
      Eating its flesh
         Feasting on its brains

Gluttonous
Without mercy

She's on her death bed
      Certain in her faith

They crawl
      further in
      deeper and deeper

            —Bill Fackler

An Ode to Allergies

I grope my way
to the medicine
cabinet
behind the mirror
Sine-aid Sudafed
Contac Dristan
Drixoral Benedryl
Allerest Actifed
down a double dose
I feel like Betty Ford
allergies
forsake me please
and leave
yesterday
eight sneezes
in a row
(someone said
you die
after seven)
if it's the
devil inside
that I'm
letting out
(I don't expect you
to bless me
each time either)
I'd rather
be possessed
than congested
why I don't
dare smell
daisies or roses
that poisonous
pollen will
penetrate
my nasal passages

fall is not
falling fast
enough
enough enough
of these

respiratory
embarrassments
and Mother Nature
you're not helping
by refusing to rain
instead whipping
that dreadful
yellow film
off spruce pine
aspen oak
ragweed
and cottonwood
into your
once winsome
now wicked wind
alleviate this
atopy idoblapsis
anon
these purple
crescents beneath
my eyes
are rather
unbecoming
there'll be no
romping and rolling
in a golden field
for me
it's intoxicating
in more than
one way
I'm afraid

ACHOO
that's it
I've had it
I'm heading
west
to the coast
to recapture
the rapture
of the
sea
set sail
on the Pacific

a mistress
of the open
waters
where not
a spot of
land is
in sight
out of reach
of anything
green
or germinating
call me on
the marine radio
when at last
the first snows
fly and the
dour dust
the frigging flour
of flowers
that damn
plant sperm
is finally
frigid in winter's
grasp.
         —Rebecca Bush

Other Ideas
for Teaching and Writing

by Ron Padgett

Here, in no particular order, are some other ideas for using Whitman in the classroom.

Interlinear Collaborations

Copy, or have students copy, lines from *Leaves of Grass*, leaving blank spaces between the lines, and then have the students write lines of their own in the blanks. The result is a "collaborative" poem by Whitman and students in alternating lines.

The result can be quite good, because Whitman's baggy style leaves a lot of room for additions. Having students try the same exercise, but working from a tighter original (such as one of Shakespeare's sonnets) is instructive: it's much harder and the result is usually less satisfying.

Faces

Kenneth Koch's poem "Faces" is a good example of how one poet can directly inspire another. His poem comes from Whitman's poem of the same name. Here's an excerpt from Koch's:

The face of the gypsy watching the bird gun firing into the colony of seals; but it was filled with blanks;
The face of the old knoll watching his hills grow up before him;
The face of the New England fruit juice proprietor watching his whole supplies being overturned by a herd of wild bulls;
The face of a lemur watching the other primates become more developed;
The face of gold, as the entire world goes on the silver standard, but gold remains extremely valuable and is the basis for international exchange;
The face of the sky, as the air becomes increasingly filled with smoke and planes;
The face of the young girl painted as Saint Urbana by Perugino, whose large silver eyes are focused on the green pomegranate held by a baby (it is Jesus) in the same painting;

The face of the sea after there has been a storm, and the face of the valley
When the clouds have blown away and it is going to be a pleasant day
  and the pencils come out for their picnic;
The face of the clouds;
The faces of the targets when all the arrows are sticking out of them, like
  tongues [. . .]

(From The Pleasures of Peace)

    Whitman's and Koch's poems are actually quite different. Whitman's is philosophical and metaphoric; Koch's is an imaginative (and sometimes comic) explosion. Both have variety of pace, tone, and description.

    Present Whitman's poem (or part of it) to your students and, before they write "faces" poems of their own, have them think about the great variety of faces they have seen, of people and things, real and imagined. You can get a Whitmanic effect by reading aloud all the faces poems as if they formed one big poem.

Zooms

Give students Whitman's little poem, "A Farm Picture":

Through the ample open door of the peaceful country barn,
A sunlit pasture field with cattle and horses feeding,
And haze and vista, and the far horizon fading away.

    Point out (or allow students to point out) its cinematic sweep, from close up to the far distance—from barn door out to pasture to vista to far horizon. You might even sketch the scene on the board. Have students form their own mental picture of a real or imagined scene and use a "zoom" similar to Whitman's. The zoom could be either in or out. The scene might include sounds and smells, too.

Escape to the Real

The general idea of Whitman's poem "I Heard the Learn'd Astronomer" is one that young people agree with: how much better is the real thing than a lot of grown-up palaver about it:

When I heard the learn'd astronomer,
When the proofs, the figures, were ranged in columns before me,
When I was shown the charts and diagrams, to add, divide, and measure
   them,
When I sitting heard the astronomer where he lectured with much
   applause in the lecture-room,
How soon unaccountable I became tired and sick,
Till rising and gliding out I wander'd off by myself,
In the mystical moist night-air, and from time to time,
Look'd up in perfect silence at the stars.

The poem's structure is simple, a series of When clauses followed
by a resolution. Ask students to write about a time (or times)
when they were in a place they didn't want to be (dentist's chair,
roomful of boring adults, etc.), and to describe leaving and being
elsewhere. Make sure they include details. If they want, they can
use Whitman's "When . . . when . . . when . . . when . . . (until) . . ."
structure or a variation on it.

Printer's Shop

Take students on a field trip to a printer's shop. Many towns,
even some small ones, still have a job printer who sets type by
hand. Ask the printer to explain the whole process of setting
type, pulling proofs, and running off the final job. It's the same
process Whitman went through in putting out *Leaves of Grass*.
Back at school, have the students do the same with their own
writing, using a rubber stamp kit (available at good stationery
shops). Then, if possible, have them "set their own type" on a
word processor.

Marathon Reading

Marathon readings are not for everyone, though they are perfect
for Whitman's work. The idea simply is to read his poetry aloud
for a long time. You might want to propose it to your students as
a kind of Guinness Book of World Records challenge. It's best if
the students read in relays: most people's voices give out during
the approximately three hours it takes to read "Song of Myself"

184

aloud. As the reading progresses, the listeners tend to tune in and tune out; the mind wanders away, comes back, goes on trains of thought parallel to those of the poem, gets bored, suddenly wakes up, notices new things in the poem, etc. Sometimes, as is the case with long-distance runners who get their second wind, the listener will make a breakthrough into feeling that it is possible to listen to this poem forever.

Punctuation

The punctuation in the first edition of *Leaves of Grass* is freewheeling. Whitman made liberal use of dashes and ellipses, which tend to keep the writing open and moving forward. (Incidentally, the dominant punctuation mark in the manuscripts of the other great nineteenth-century American poet, Emily Dickinson, is the dash.)

Give your students a sample from the early Whitman—or invent one yourself—that uses lots of dashes—or ellipses—or both. As an experiment, have everyone write without using any other form of punctuation—in many cases the writing will be freer and bolder than usual and at least will help students get a better feel for Whitman's poetry.

The Adventures of Whitman

by Dave Morice

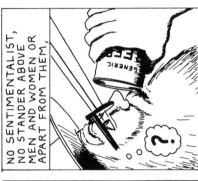

NO SENTIMENTALIST, NO STANDER ABOVE MEN AND WOMEN OR APART FROM THEM,

TURBULENT, FLESHY, SENSUAL, EATING, DRINKING AND BREEDING,

THE ADVENTURES OF

IT'S A BARD.... IT'S A POET.... IT'S ....

WALT WHITMAN, A KOSMOS, OF MANHATTAN, THE SON,

FROM PAUMANOK STARTING I FLY LIKE A BIRD,

UNSCREW THE LOCKS FROM THEIR DOORS! UNSCREW THE DOORS THEMSELVES FROM THEIR JAMBS!

NO MORE MODEST THAN IMMODEST,

187

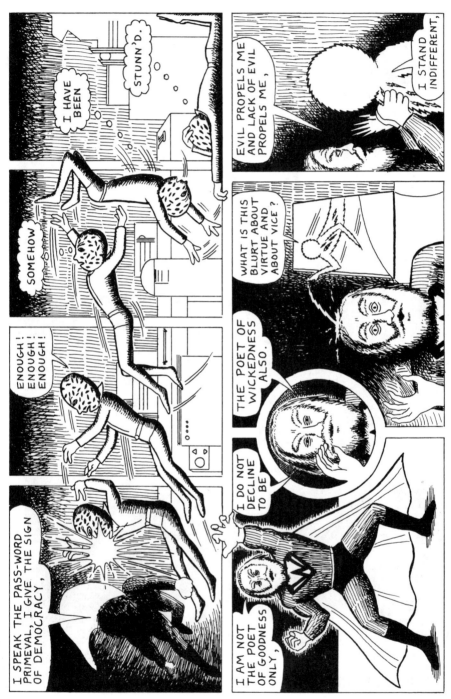

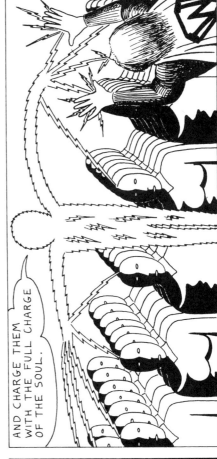

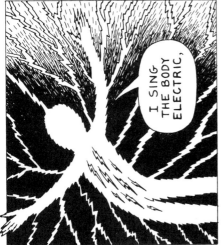

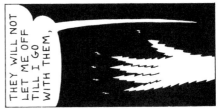

Brief Chronology

1819	Born May 31 at West Hills, near Huntington, Long Island
1823	Whitman family moves to Brooklyn.
1825–30	Attends public schools.
1830–34	Learns about printing.
1835	Works as a printer.
1836–38	Teaches at rural schools on Long Island.
1838–41	Edits the Huntington *Long Islander* newspaper; teaches; works in Van Buren presidential campaign; teaches.
1841	Works as printer in New York City.
1842–48	Writes for and edits various New York and Brooklyn newspapers.
1848	Goes to New Orleans to work for the *New Orleans Crescent.*
1848–49	Edits the *Brooklyn Freeman.*
1850–54	Operates a printing office and stationery store; writes freelance; does building contracting and speculates in real estate.
1855	Publishes first edition of *Leaves of Grass* in early July. Father dies July 11.
1856	Publishes second edition of *Leaves of Grass.*
1857–59	Edits the *Brooklyn Times.*

1860	Goes to Boston to oversee publication of third edition of *Leaves of Grass*.
1862	Goes to Virginia to visit brother wounded in Civil War.
1863–64	Stays in Washington, D.C., working in Army Paymaster's Office; visits wounded in hospitals; returns to Brooklyn when he falls ill.
1865	Works as clerk for Deptartment of the Interior. Pub-lishes "Drum-Taps" section of *Leaves of Grass*. Fired by Interior Secretary Harlan, who finds *Leaves of Grass* indecent. Immediately hired by Attorney General's office. Publishes *Sequel to Drum-Taps*.
1867	Publishes fourth edition of *Leaves of Grass*.
1868	In London, *Poems by Walt Whitman* is published.
1870–71	Publishes fifth edition of *Leaves of Grass* in two printings, the second revised. Publishes *Democratic Vistas*.
1872	Reads at Dartmouth College commencement and at National Industrial Exposition in New York.
1873	Suffers paralytic stroke January 23. Mother dies May 23. Goes to live with brother George in Camden, New Jersey.
1876	Publishes sixth edition of *Leaves of Grass*; be-gins visits to Stafford farm (near Timber Creek in New Jersey).
1879	Delivers the first of his Lincoln lectures; goes to Colorado (the "Western jaunt"); his illness

causes him to stay three months with brother Jeff in St. Louis.

1880   Visits his disciple Dr. R. M. Bucke in Canada.

1881–82   Publishes seventh edition of *Leaves of Grass* twice because first publisher, fearing prosecution, stops distributing it; publishes *Specimen Days and Collect*.

1884   Buys house at unfashionable 330 Mickle St., Camden.

1888   Suffers paralytic stroke. *Complete Poems and Prose of Walt Whitman* published.

1889   Publishes eighth edition of *Leaves of Grass*.

1892   Ninth edition of *Leaves of Grass* (the so-called "deathbed edition") published. Dies March 26; buried in Harleigh Cemetery, Camden.

Whitman Resources

by Ron Padgett

If an entry below has no comment, it means we at Teachers & Writers have not examined it, and therefore are not necessarily recommending it. The prices are current as of 1991.

Editions

Whitman, Walt. *The Collected Writings*, eds. Gay Wilson Allen and Sculley Bradley (New York: New York University Press). This 22-volume set is in progress. Check for current status.

_____. *Leaves of Grass*, eds. Sculley Bradley and Harold W. Blodgett (New York: W. W. Norton, 1973), sometimes called the Norton Critical Edition, follows the text of the "deathbed" edition (the final one authorized by Whitman), has good footnotes explaining arcane words and references, and includes unpublished poems and manuscript fragments. $15.95.

_____. *Leaves of Grass* (New York: Bantam Books, 1983), ed. Justin Kaplan. The 1892 text, with an introduction by Kaplan. $3.50.

_____. *Leaves of Grass* (New York: New American Library, 1980), ed. Gay Wilson Allen. The 1892 text, with an introduction by Allen. $3.50.

_____. *The Complete Poems* (New York: Penguin, 1989), ed. Frances Murphy. This 892-page paperback includes the 1892 text of *Leaves of Grass*, poems Whitman excluded from it, early poems, the first edition of *Leaves*, Whitman's prefaces to the various editions, and Murphy's valuable notes. A bargain at $8.95.

_____. *Complete Poetry and Collected Prose* (New York: The Library of America, 1982), ed. Justin Kaplan. There's a lot of Whitman here, but some of the publisher's claims are untrue:

this volume does not contain Whitman's complete poetry, nor is it the only volume that reproduces the 1855 edition of *Leaves of Grass*. $30 hardcover.

_____. *Leaves of Grass* (New York: Eakins Press Foundation, 1966). If you'd like to give yourself (or someone else) a special present, order this beautiful facsimile of the first edition of *Leaves of Grass*. The Eakins Foundation Press, 15 W. 67th St., New York, NY 10023. Telephone (212) 496-2255. Teachers receive a 20% discount off the $50 retail price, so the total cost is $40, which includes shipping and handling.

_____. *The Essential Whitman*, ed. Galway Kinnell (New York: Ecco Press, 1987). Something in me resists being told what is "essential" in any writer, but that is a problem with the name of the series (*The Essential Keats, The Essential Milton*, etc.) in which this book appears. The book itself is attractive and personable, the selection of poems good. The editor, Galway Kinnell, is a poet himself, and he has done something radical in this edition. In some cases, he has taken part of a poem from one edition and another part from another edition, creating "versions that have never existed before." $6.

_____. *The Portable Walt Whitman* (New York: Penguin, 1973), ed. Mark Van Doren. For readers seeking generous selections of Whitman's poetry and prose and a good introduction, all at a reasonable price, this is the single best edition to buy. Includes a bibliography and chronology. $9.95.

_____. *An American Primer* (Stevens Point, WI: Holy Cow! Press, 1987). A photographic reprint of the Whitman essay on the American language, originally brought out in 1904 by one of his disciples, Horace Traubel. This handsome edition includes an afterword by Gay Wilson Allen. Available in hardcover ($10 plus $1 shipping) or paperback ($5 plus $.50 shipping) from the Walt Whitman Quarterly Review, Department of English, 308 EPB, The University of Iowa, Iowa City, IA 52242.

(The following three books are for children.)

_____. *Overhead the Sun: Lines from Walt Whitman* (New York: Farrar, Straus & Giroux, 1969). Supposedly for grade 3 and up, these brief selections sound like poems about childhood for adults. Or perhaps they simply provide an occasion for Antonio Frasconi's pretty woodcuts that illustrate them.

_____. *Voyages* (New York: Harcourt Brace Jovanovich, 1988), ed. Lee Bennett Hopkins. This selection for grade 4 and up demonstrates the difficulty (impossibility?) of selecting Whitman for children's books. Too many of the poems here are short and homiletic, Whitman far from his best. Also, a desexualized Whitman just isn't as interesting. Even the good selection in Deutsch's biography (see below), which includes longer poems, is required to delete the erotic passages.

_____. *Poems of Walt Whitman: Leaves of Grass Selected* (New York: Thomas Y. Crowell, 1964), ed. Lawrence Clark Powell. Apparently for grade 4 and up.

Biographies

Allen, Gay Wilson. *The Solitary Singer: A Critical Biography of Walt Whitman* (Chicago: University of Chicago Press, 1985). Originally published in 1955 and still one of the best biographies of Whitman.

Deutsch, Babette. *Walt Whitman, Builder for America* (New York: Julian Messner, 1941). This is the kind of biography for young people (grade 4 and up) that was more common 50 years ago: knowledgeable, detailed, lengthy, and believable. The biographical text (178 pp.) is followed by 100 pages of Whitman's poetry, with a guide showing how the two sections can be correlated.

Kaplan, Justin. *Walt Whitman: A Life* (New York: Simon & Schuster, 1980). A solid, enjoyable, and serious popular biography of the poet. Highly recommended.

Marinaci, Barbara. *O Wondrous Singer!* (New York: Dodd,

Mead, 1970). We haven't seen this one, but the title is not very encouraging.

Miller, James E., Jr. *Walt Whitman* (New York: Twayne, 1962). For grade 6 and up. Not seen by us.

Stoutenberg, Adrien and Laura Nelson. *Listen, America* (New York: Scribner's, 1968). We haven't seen this biography for children.

Criticism and Homages

Allen, Gay Wilson. *The New Walt Whitman Handbook* (New York: New York University Press, 1975) is a valuable book with a particularly good section on the subject of Whitman's effect on world literature.

_____. *Walt Whitman* (Detroit: Wayne State Univ. Press, 1969) includes a brief biography, very brief excerpts from Whitman, very brief critical responses, and good period illustrations.

Jaén, Didier Tisdel. *Homage to Walt Whitman: a Collection of Poems from the Spanish* (Tuscaloosa, AL: University of Alabama Press, 1969). A bilingual collection of poems about Whitman by Jorge Luis Borges, Léon Felipe, Leopoldo Lugones, Rubén Darío, Ezequiel Martínez Estrada, Alfredo Cardona Peña, Federico García Lorca, Pedro Mir, and Pablo Neruda. Foreword by Borges, and as an appendix, José Martí's pioneering 1887 essay on Whitman. Although some of the translations are a little flat, this is a trim little collection.

Kummings, Donald D., ed. *Approaches to Teaching Whitman's* Leaves of Grass (New York: Modern Language Association of America, 1990). This collection of essays for college teachers contains an excellent bibliographical essay by the editor, as well as fine pieces by Ed Folsom and Alan Helms that describe how the structures of their upper-level seminars on Whitman actually mirrored the work being studied. Martin

Bidney's brief essay on Whitman's prosody is innovative and clear. Doris Sommer's "Bard of Both Americas" tells us, among other interesting things, that in 1969 Jorge Luis Borges "published an exquisite, but selective, translation of *Leaves of Grass* and dedicated it to Richard Nixon." To order copies of this book (192 pp., $19 paper, $34 cloth, ouch!), write MLA Customer Services, 10 Astor Place, New York, NY 10003-6981, or call (212) 614-6384.

Perlman, Jim, Ed Folsom, and Dan Campion, eds. *Walt Whitman: The Measure of His Song* (Minneapolis: Holy Cow! Press, 1981) is an invaluable and exemplary 394-page collection of poets' responses to Whitman, from Emerson's famous 1855 letter to a 1980 essay by Meridel LeSueur. In between are many high points and surprises. For current ordering information, write to Holy Cow! Press, P.O. Box 3170, Mount Royal Station, Duluth, MN 55803.

Bibliographies

Two standard bibliographies of Whitman provide annotated year-by-year lists of more than 8,000 items: *Walt Whitman, 1838–1939: A Reference Guide* by Scott Giantvalley and *Walt Whitman, 1940–1975: A Reference Guide* by Donald D. Kummings. For bibliographies of material after 1975, see *The Walt Whitman Quarterly Review*. For shorter bibliographies, see Justin Kaplan's Bantam edition of *Leaves of Grass* or Mark Van Doren's *Portable Walt Whitman*.

Magazines

Cobblestone, the history magazine for children in grades 4–7, keeps in print its special back issue on Whitman (May 1986, Vol. 7, No. 5), with brief, illustrated articles about Whitman's youth, birthday, career as journalist, Civil War service, etc. Single copies are available for $3.95 plus $1.50 shipping. Cobblestone Publishing, 7 School Street, Peterborough, NH 03458, tel. (603) 924-7209.

The Mickle Street Review, P.O. Box 1493, Camden, NJ 08101. The annual publication of the Walt Whitman Association. Free with membership in the Walt Whitman Association (below).

The Walt Whitman Quarterly Review, 308 EPB, The University of Iowa, Iowa City, IA 52242, includes articles, book reviews, and bibliographical updates. The articles tend to be clear and interesting, but are for people with a special interest in Whitman. One-year subscriptions are $12 for individuals, $15 for institutions.

West Hills Review: A Walt Whitman Journal is devoted both to Whitman scholarship and to contemporary poetry. For more information, write to the Walt Whitman Birthplace Association, 246 Old Walt Whitman Rd., Huntington Station, NY 11746.

Films & Videos

The Living Tradition (film, with additional audiocassette and teacher's guide). For junior high-junior college levels. Centre Productions, 1800 30th St., Boulder, CO 80301.

Voices and Visions: Walt Whitman. A one-hour videocassette for high school–adult levels. From the very popular PBS series. For ordering information, call (800) LEARNER. A series *Viewer's Guide* (77 pp., $1 to cover postage) by Joseph Parisi is available from the Center for Visual History, 625 Broadway, New York, NY 10012, Attn. Alan Abrams.

Walt Whitman (Endlessly Rocking), 1986, a 21-minute film (or video) for junior high–adult levels, and *Walt Whitman: Poet for a New Age,* 1972, a 30-minute film for senior high and older. The rather bizarre *Walt Whitman (Endlessly Rocking)* depicts a class of "average" high school students who are resistant to studying Whitman. Shazam! Walt himself (portrayed by Canadian poet bp Nichol) appears atop the teacher's desk. It turns out that the students don't like his poetry because they can't dance to it. Walt, the students, and the teacher go into a rap version of "Out of the Cradle Endlessly Rocking." The students are won over. Walt says good-bye and disappears. The film ends with the students entering into a lively discussion. Available from the Syracuse University Classroom Film/Video Rental Center, 1455 Colvin St., Syracuse, NY 13244-5150. For information, call (800) 345-6797 in New York State, (800) 223-2409 in others.

Walt Whitman. A good short introduction to Whitman that makes use of period photos (and, curiously, photographs and film clips from the 1920s and 1930s), Civil War scenes from *The Birth of a Nation*, and humorous animated touches that illustrate Whitman's free verse. A videocassette in the "Against the Odds" series. Twelve minutes, color (1983). Films for the Humanities, Box 2053, Princeton, NJ 08543.

Audio Recordings

In 1991 a recording, said to be of the voice of Whitman, was released. Based on an Edison cylinder recording from around 1890, it was clarified in a modern sound studio by Prof. Lowell Cross of the University of Iowa. The reading was of the first four lines of Whitman's poem "America." Sceptics call the recording a hoax. Hoax or not, it is fun to hear. For more information, contact the Academy of American Poets at (212) 274-0343.

Galway Kinnell Reads Walt Whitman. One cassette. The contemporary poet gives good, firm, clear readings from "Song of Myself" and other poems. The best recording we know of. Unfortunately it's out of print, but sometimes available via the Internet.

Treasury of Walt Whitman: Leaves of Grass. Two cassettes. Reading by actor Alexander Scourby. Scourby's gorgeous voice sometimes gets in the way. Available from The Musical Heritage Society, 1710 Highway 35, Ocean, NJ 07712, tel. (908) 531-7000.

Walt Whitman: Eyewitness to the Civil War. Two cassettes, read by actor Ed Begley. *Walt Whitman's Leaves of Grass*, two cassettes, also read by Begley. Caedmon, c/o HarperCollins, 10 E. 53rd St., New York, NY 10022.

Photographs

Photographs of Whitman, his relatives, and his milieux are scattered throughout the many books on him.

However, all the known photographs of Whitman are reproduced in a special double issue ("This Heart's Geography's Map") of the *Walt Whitman Quarterly Review*, Vol. 4 Nos. 2/3, available for $7 plus $1 shipping from Walt Whitman Quarterly Review, Dept. of English, 308 EPB, The University of Iowa, Iowa City, IA 52242.

The photograph on the cover of the book you are holding is available in a lovely 8 x 10 black and white glossy print from The National Archives Trust Fund, (NNSP), National Archives Trust Fund Board, PO Box 100793, Atlanta, GA 30384 for $5.25, which includes shipping. The photo is also available in poster form, but only as part of the "Mathew Brady Portfolio of Eminent Americans" (Item #502, 12 posters for $10) from the National Archives in Washington, DC. Call (202) 724-0456 for more information.

Places to Visit

Walt Whitman House, the 1810 farmhouse (now museum) where Whitman spent the first four years of his life. Open all year; Wed.–Fri. 1-4, Sat. and Sun. 10–4. Closed holidays. Free admission. School and group tours by appointment. Walt Whitman House, 246 Old Walt Whitman Rd., Huntington Station, NY 11746, tel. (516) 427-5240.

The Walt Whitman House at 330 Mickle St., Camden, NJ, is where Whitman spent the last eight years of his life. For information on visits to the House, which is overseen by the State of New Jersey, call (609) 964-5383 or (609) 726-1191.

A few doors down is the Walt Whitman Association, 326 Mickle St. The Association has a library that includes original manuscripts, letters, first editions, and photographs of Whitman. Visits are by appointment. Membership in the Association

Whitman Resources

includes *Conversations*, a quarterly newsletter, and *Mickle Street Review*, an annual magazine. For more information, contact the Walt Whitman Association at P.O. Box 1493, Camden, NJ 08101, tel. (609) 541-8280.

The Whitman tomb, designed by Walt himself, holds not only the poet, but also his mother, father, two brothers, a sister, and a sister-in-law. Not far from the Walt Whitman House, Harleigh Cemetery, at 1640 Haddon Ave. in Camden, NJ (off Rt. 130), is open from 7:30-4:30 daily. Signs direct visitors to the tomb, which is not far from the front gate. For more information, call (609) 963-0122.

Available from The Academy of American Poets is their guidebook *Four Literary-Historical Walks* by Elizabeth Kray. Two of the walks follow Whitman through lower Manhattan (the other two walks are for Poe and Melville). The guidebook is clear and informative and includes good maps and attractive illustrations; it's fun to read even if you aren't taking the walks. The reasonable $7 price includes shipping. The Academy of American Poets, 177 E. 87th St., New York, NY 10028, tel. (212) 427-5665.

Among the South Street Seaport Museum's many programs is an ongoing workshop, "Ink, Roll, and Pull," that introduces students in grades 4–12 to letterpress printing, the kind of printing Whitman used to produce *Leaves of Grass*. Call M.J. Shaughnessy at the number below for details. Bowne & Co., the Museum's print shop, offers publications relevant to Whitman: "Manahatta," a broadside of his poem of the same name ($5 plus $1 shipping), and *A Visit to the Printer*, a little booklet that describes letterpress printing ($1.25 plus 35¢ shipping). South Street Seaport Museum, 207 Front St., New York, NY 10038, tel. (212) 669-9400.

Contributors

JIM BERGER is a poet who taught poetry writing in the T&W program for three years and who taught third grade in Tanzania. He is currently working on a Ph.D. in English from the University of Virginia.

JACK COLLOM has published seven books of poems. T&W published his *Moving Windows: Evaluating the Poetry Children Write*. He has received two NEA Fellowships in Poetry.

MARGOT FORTUNATO GALT is a poet and teacher. Her poems have appeared in many magazines, and two of her plays have been produced. She is currently writing *The Story in History*, a book about teaching writing and history.

LARRY FAGIN has taught poetry to children since 1969. In 1980 he received an NEA Fellowship in Poetry. In addition to thirteen books of poetry, he is the author of *The List Poem: A Guide to Writing Catalog Verse* (T&W).

ALLEN GINSBERG's *Collected Poems* was published by Harper & Row. He teaches writing at Brooklyn College and at Naropa Institute's School of Disembodied Poetics, which he co-founded.

LANGSTON HUGHES (1902-1967) published many books of poetry, fiction, and commentary. His *Selected Poems* is available from Vintage Books. Like Whitman, he is the subject of one of the *Voices & Visions* PBS programs.

KENNETH KOCH is a poet who teaches at Columbia University. He is the author of *Wishes, Lies, and Dreams* and other books about teaching poetry writing. Random House published his *Selected Poems*.

GARY LENHART's books include *Bulb in Socket* and *Light Heart* (Hanging Loose Press). He is Associate Director of T&W and the editor of *Transfer* magazine.

WILLIAM BRYANT LOGAN is a poet, essayist, and translator. Recipient of an NEH translation fellowship and writer in residence at New York's Cathedral of St. John the Divine, he translated Lorca's play *Once Five Years Pass* (Station Hill Press).

DAVE MORICE is a poet and artist who has also written children's books. Simon & Schuster published his *Poetry Comics* and T&W published his *How to Make Poetry Comics*. He teaches at the University of Iowa.

RON PADGETT is T&W's Publications Director. His poetry books include *The Big Something* and *Great Balls of Fire*. For T&W he edited the *Handbook of Poetic Forms*. He is the translator of *The Complete Poems of Blaise Cendrars*.

MARK STATMAN's poetry, fiction, and criticism have appeared in *The Village Voice*, *The Columbia Review*, and other magazines. He has received fellowships from the NEA and the National Writers Project. He has taught writing since 1984.

ANNE WALDMAN is a poet and director of the writing program at Naropa Institute. Her many books include *Fast Speaking Woman* (City Lights). She performs her work across America and Europe.

DALE WORSLEY is a fiction writer and playwright. Mabou Mines/The New York Shakespeare Festival produced his play *Cold Harbor*, which toured Europe. He co-authored *The Art of Science Writing* (T&W).

BILL ZAVATSKY is a poet who teaches English at Trinity School in New York. He co-edited *The Whole Word Catalogue 2* (Teachers & Writers/McGraw-Hill). His other books include *Theories of Rain* (SUN) and a translation of Valery Larbaud.